A Light in the Darkness

A Light in the Darkness

Inspirational Christian Poetry

Regina McIntosh

Foreword by Sheila Ramsey

RESOURCE *Publications* · Eugene, Oregon

A LIGHT IN THE DARKNESS
Inspirational Christian Poetry

Resource Publications
An Imprint of Wipf and Stock Publishers
199 W. 8th Ave., Suite 3
Eugene, OR 97401

www.wipfandstock.com

PAPERBACK ISBN: 978-1-6667-9169-3
HARDCOVER ISBN: 978-1-6667-9168-6
EBOOK ISBN: 978-1-6667-9170-9

DECEMBER 8, 2021 8:37 AM

I want to thank my beautiful and talented mother, Norma Arrowood, who was the one to show instead of tell me how to love like Jesus does! May He always bring her joy, hope and peace that surpasses understanding.

I want to thank the many family members, church family and friends who have supported and encouraged me over the years in my yearning to write from the heart.

I also want to thank my husband, Morris McIntosh, for being so supportive and kind, with a heart of pure gold and always a inspiration for my words. I love him beyond words!

And, I'd especially like to thank my Lord and Savior, JESUS CHRIST, who has blessed me more than I could possibly imagine. He is my everything and I love Him more than anything! He is truly my greatest inspiration!

Thank you so much for reading these poems

Contents

Foreword

THE NATIONAL NEWS BLARES a world wide warning of increased natural disasters, rising energy costs, climate in crisis, shortages and rising cost of food, companies declaring bankruptcy as the Covid pandemic continues to take lives and affect every family worldwide.

I believe we are living in the last days of Creation, as the End of Time is nearing as prophesied in Matthew 24:7 (KJV): "for nation shall rise against nation, and kingdom against kingdom: and there shall be famines, and pestilences, and earthquakes, in divers places."

As we watch and wait for the glorious coming of our Lord and Savior, we must encourage and minister to the needs of each other. This book of poetry, "A Light in the Darkness" by Regina McIntosh, will encourage, strengthen faith and bring peace and joy to the reader.

I met this Christian poetess on the first day of school as she came into my second grade classroom. Sporting a new purple dress with matching hairbows, she walked with a bounce of enthusiasm that gave the head full of natural curls freedom to spring like corkscrews, framing her large September sky-blue eyes. Her pursed little lips gave way to a heart-melting smile that revealed new white teeth with a space between the front incisors. She was interested in two main learning centers: art and writing!

Gina was the class catalyst as she chose to write about the things she knew. Living beneath the shadow of the John King Mountain in the Appalachian chain of Yancey County, NC, she saw wildlife and nature's creation visible to only a few who are fortunate enough to live among such splendor. Reared in a Christian home, with a loving family, Gina was never without paper, pencils and the beauty of nature and God's word to capture and create visions in poetic form for others to enjoy.

Continuing to write, this poetess has written professionally for others who published her works. God recently placed a yearning in her heart to use this gift He has given her to bring honor and glory to His Holy name. Reading her work stirs the soul... rekindling fires of hope, reminding us of God's Amazing Grace as it takes our thought from the darkness we are experiencing in these days of crisis and renews our faith in God and His promises as we press "Homeward".

Sheila Dianne Pate Ramsey
Retired Teacher and Principal
Bee Log Elementary School
Yancey County, Burnsville, NC

God Breathed

God breathed
      Hope across my soul
Music into my thoughts
      Joy all over my heart

God breathed
      Laughter into my mind
Pleasure on my ideas
      Kindness across my feelings

God breathed
      Inspiration over my plans
Harmony into my designs
      Sighs of love on my spirit

God breathed
      Wonders across my beliefs
Miracles to whisper praise
      Admiration into my faith

God breathed
      Satisfaction on my essence
Gladness across my dreams
      Poetry into my allegiance

God breathed
      Insight into my strength
Purpose over my reveries
      A song over my mood

God breathed
      Courage onto my character
Marvels over my delight
      Enlightenment into the night

God breathed
>Tenderness through my judgements
Affection onto my generosity
>A light that leaves me encouraged

God breathed
>A promise that heartens my attitude
A devotion that colors me brilliant
>A wisdom in the center of my giving

God breathed
>Warmth over my yearnings
Gentleness onto my provision
>Compassion through my personality

God breathed
>Stardust through my vision
Pearls of ecstasy on my depths
>Assurance of His eternal love

God breathed
>And I existed
God breathed
>And I listened
God breathed
>And I worshipped

A Light

There is a light
Surrounding the soul
Like laughter and love
Calming and joyful
Sweetening thoughts
With inspiring
Smiles

There is a light
Caressing and clean
Falling all around us
Like grace so gentle
Coloring the air
In whispery
Praise

There is a light
Delighting with insight
Rhythms and rhymes
Poetry on the wind
Dancing with dreams
Piercing the dark
Embracing

There is light
Wonders of hope
Pouring from the heavens
Like rain, so soothing
Dews of exhilaration
Flooded imagination
Serenity

There is light
Flooding the night
With stardust thoughts
Images of moonbeams
Awakening prayers
To assurance
Belief

There is light
Singing in the sky
Glorifying His Son
The One who knows us
Loves without conditions
Gives the gift of
Freedom

I know Him
I praise Him
I love Him

Death

I know he will die
Someday
Everyone dies
At least
That's what they say

Everyone dies
Or do they?

My heart pounds
Rhythmic like raindrops
Pouring out into the sea
Small beads of moisture
Crimson in veins thirsty
For music or vibrant hues
Of laughter, love
Smiling

My soul sings
In racing velocity
Speeding through the day
Like a whisper of faith
Flows tenderness
Praise and prayer
Grace, inspiration
Worship

I know he will die
There is no mystery
Everyone who lives must die
And he too will go someday
From whatever ailment
Weaves its way through him
Polluting his memory

With pain and grief
Anguish that fades
Into the loss
Adrift

When he goes
And I know he won't be coming home
There will be flowers placed
A wreath on the door
Foreboding yet hopeful
In our prayers
He must be waiting
At heaven's gate
Pearly gates
Home

His passing
Will bring peace
Because we know, eternity
Holds the key to his fate
And with God in control
With Jesus as his savior
There is only assurance
Grace and peace
Salvation
Reigns

He will die someday
But there is the promise
That his death
Will bring him home
And we need not worry
God holds the soul
In His open palm
Forever alive
Surviving

Death and it's darkness
Are wounded by the light
That is like a fiery blaze
Bringing love from the
Shadows, the black
That seems to grow
From death's
Anguish

God's love frees our soul
Even from death
And I am thankful
That I know His grace
Will bring me face to face
With His Son
The One I truly love!

I know he will die
And so will I
But Jesus is alive
To meet me in a sky
Where I will one day
Fly

His Light

His light shines
Surrounding me with hope
Everlasting love
Peace that keeps me
Assured of the victory

His light glows bright
Encompassing me with joy
Amazing grace so sweet
Gentle flow of song
Whispered on the heart

His light sparkles
Radiating a tenderness
Kindness so vibrant
It feels like adoration
Breathing pleasure

His light glimmers
Enfolding me with stillness
Silence that believes
Enriches hearts with faith
Assuring with praise

His light glitters
Enclosing me with calm
Certainty that He is alive
Giving hope to every life
Answering prayers

His light twinkles
Enveloping me in compassion
Soothing away all sorrow

Brightening thoughts with surety
Singing silent relief

His light shimmers
Hedging me with protection
Securing my direction
With wonder that is accepting
Of every supplication

His light glistens
Girding me with armor
From the God who is always
There to guide me through the storm
Piercing the dark with His love

He Knows Me

He knows my heart
My every thought
He sees my worst fear
Listens to my prayers
Even when I'm wrong
He never leaves me alone

He knows my soul
The air I breathe is His gift
He isn't surprised
When I learn my lesson
Or even when
I can't prevail and fail again

He knows my needs
Before I even dream them
He holds me up
Without Him, I would surely
Fall through the cracks
Never to be found

He knows my feelings
Reads my ideas
He fills my heart up
With inspiration and joy
Assurance that I know
Comes from His quickening

He knows my fears
The ones I refuse to voice
He strengthens me
And leads me toward true freedom
Where I can be spontaneous
Alive with creativity and imagination

He knows my yearnings
As I pray for His will to be done
He sees what I want
Even when I don't pray at all
And He lifts me up
So that I can have the best there is

He delights in my joy
Assures me that I'm more
Important than I know
He even allows me to grow
Wiser with time
More alive – so I shine!

He knows me better
Than I know myself
He inspires my finest efforts
With His blessings, His love
The assurance that He is there
Protecting me, accepting me

He knows me and I know Him
He is love and He is my friend
With God by my side
I know I'll gain the victory
He is the answer to my prayer
For love that is always there

Blessings

Sunlight pours through the window
Caressing my thoughts so intimately
A gentle whisper of God's affection
Soothing, illuminating His direction

Rain falls soft on my soul, praying
For the kind rainbow after the storm
Delighting, exciting, raising up hope
For another day, a new way, tomorrow

Roses, lilacs, dandelions too . . .
Rise up from the earth, nourished
By the light of sun, the rain's love
Brightening lives with their blooms

Moon, stars, fireflies too . . .
Bursting through the darkness
Coloring the night in hues of dreams
Silencing the flames of failure and doubt

Robin and wren, butterflies so wild . . .
Paint the morning in psalms of joy
Inspiration that awakens the mercies
Of laughter sung across the rise of dawn

Dewdrops slide like elastic grace
Across a petal, a leaf, a spider's web
Imagining the night where it grew to be
The miracle of beauty breathing intimately

Kindness cascades down my life
Inspiring me to believe, to reach out
To give generously and intentionally
With love that showers me with sensitivity

My blessings never cease to be cherished
As treasures for which I am so thankful
God is the best giver and His gifts are
Bigger than any that we might give

His gifts come from the very hope
That awakens His passion for bounteous giving
I've never felt so blessed before
And I know each day only brings more
To be thankful for – God is so good!

I need to Thank Him forevermore!

Pandemic Thoughts

As fear covers hearts
A dread so worrisome it even stops
Hopes and dreams, fantasies
Leaving only alarm and anxiety
To color the thoughts
In darkest black, shadowed by gray
Images brought to life
On storms of suffering, angst

There comes the assurance
That even in these perilous times
When sorrow and heartache
Bind plans and silence inspirations
There is One who never changes

The God I speak of is forever alive
A constant light, a source of insight
The guide of my life and the answer to strife
He makes a way where no way can be seen
He glows bright through the darkness
Where only those who believe can see

The God I pray to, the God who I praise
He assures me that everything will be fine
He fills my heart with faith and belief
He assures me that I'm worth it
Even when I don't feel like I am
He knows I need His love
And He is generous with hope
Unlike myself, this God I speak of
Is perfect and I can see
He is the answer to my every need

He colors my darkest thoughts

In light that lifts my heart
Frees me from the dread and grief
Awakens the joy inside of me
Even in these fearful times
He assures me that love can be mine!

Pandemic or not – He brings peace of mind

You're Everything To Me

With adoration
I come to You, Lord
Offering praise
And applause for your love

With admiration
I come to You, Lord
Offering worship
Devotion and celebration
You are the One
Who makes my life better

With approbation
I come to You, Lord
Offering tribute
Glory, honor and blessing
Reverence for all You are
Goodness, kindness, grace and mercy
Everything that makes life worth it!

With all my heart
I love you, dear Lord
And thank You for everything
Your blessings are eternal
You are wisdom, strength and affection
You make me feel like I can do it
Even when I'm weak and uncertain
You are the One who fills me with hope
Gives me the power to overcome the world
And reminds me that I am someone who is loved
I am God's child and that is simply enough
In a world where most are reaching out for more
God is my anchor through every storm
He is my light, my guide and my joy

He makes my life a place where I know
I can find the inspiration to do what I'm sure
Is the thing He has for me to do, the purpose
That makes my life a place I can find serenity

With all my heart – I love You, God
And with all my soul – I give to You
My sincerity, my dreams, my everything
You are the One who created me
And I know You can bring me the peace
That leaves me assured I have all I need
The hope, faith and love that is sent from above
To bring me grace that fulfills every dream

I love You, God – You're everything to me!

Psalm 138:8 (KJV) The Lord will perfect that which concerneth me: thy mercy,
O Lord, endureth for ever: forsake not the works of thine own hands.

In An Inkling

In an inkling
Sunlight flickers out
Hidden behind dark clouds
Dimming even my reflections

In an inkling
Raindrops caress my skin
Refreshing, reviving
Even my thoughts are adventures

In an inkling
Leaves in hues of green
Dance, twirling in the wind
Enlightening my wildest dreams

In an inkling
Rivers flow across smooth stones
So alive, yet so alone
Winding their way toward the sea

In an inkling
Seasons change the air
Gracing hearts with prayers
Peppering life with serenity so rare

In an inkling
Rainbows breathe hope
Painting souls in shades of glory
Gentling even the blistering sun

In an inkling
Morning rouses the spirit
Reveries capture kind feelings
Inspirations fall over nature's miracles

In an inkling
God opens the door for joy
Blessing us all with pure faith
Poured out on those who know grace

In an inkling
Love beckons the heart
Inspiring affections and thoughts
Of generosity, understanding and praise

In an inkling
My idyll thoughts flicker
With images far in the distance
Of a heaven where I can grow sweeter

In Praise of Peace

From the stillness, the quiet
The silence that falls
On the heart and soul
Whispering joy, love and hope

From the tender whisper
Of a butterfly
As it kisses a daisy
Or the moment when a
Morning dewdrop
Slides over a petal

From the breath of light
Reflected on dawn's
Soft echo

From the sigh, the whisper,
The precious glimpse
Of feeling
On God's azure sky
On the caress of a raindrop
As it plops onto my shoulder
Over the soothing air
As a gaggle of birds gather

From the heart and soul
Where only God can know
There comes a peace
That exceeds all understanding
A peace that leads me
Toward a life of gentleness
A thought of inspiration
A shadow of exaltation
Sweet prayers and praise

Come in waves as the peace
Fills me, frees me, floods me

This is peace that believes in three
The Father, Son and Holy Spirit
Given as God's generous gift to me

Philippians 4:7 (KJV) And the peace of God, which passeth all understanding, shall keep your hearts and minds through Christ Jesus.

Lift Your Eyes

His sun falls across my bare shoulders
Seeking a tender thought
Breathing light along the hopes
That gentle my mind and my heart

His moon pours a wispy affection
Across the music of my soul
Coloring me in hues of acceptance
Simple joy to my sight

His stars reflect all the shimmer
Beyond the seas and waves
Where azure laughter sinks deeper
Than the silence that fascinates

His voice caresses my spirit
With faith flowing in my veins
Creating crimson whispers
Bright as the fire's flames

His vision keeps me focused
On kindness that soothes and sustains
Capturing the dreams of forever
Inside the blazing firefly dance

His grace cascades like a waterfall
Gushing with gladness and peace
Arousing soft feelings of pleasure
Grown famous by the unending mercy

His inspiration nourishes my soul
In angel's hymns that raise my thoughts
Of joy, peace and sacred prayers
Sweet sighs of faith painting warm praises

His light guides me through the storms
Lifting the shadows that might harm
Giving my mind a chance to grow strong
With the rays of love falling from His spirit

His is a love that knows no bounds
He sends it down from the highest heavens
Illuminating and reflecting all the joy
Caught up in the soul who knows His worth

His is a grace that appeals to the senses
Guides hearts from the worst
And reveals the truth about giving unconditionally
From a heart who knows that love is the greatest gift

Lift your eyes to the highest stars
See the moon, the glow of heaven's hope
Whispering insight through your thoughts
And know that love is alive on the inside

Story of Love

Our stories are different
We travel different paths
You go toward the rainbow
While I plod a forest trail
You move through the storms
While rain leaves me feeling
Cold and alone, like I need to
Find shelter from the elements

Our stories are different
We seek a different world
You seek the light of sun and song
While I pursue a challenging thought
Melancholy assuring me that I have
All I need to reach my goals
Pass my tests and face my trials
With assurance that I abide
In the hope that colors my world
With hues of kindness and love

Our stories are different, yet
We both long for our dreams
To come to life on the end of a faith
That falls from our souls, reaching
Down toward our spirits and believing
Grace will call softly through the winds
Whispering inspiration and creativity
Singing songs of tenderness and gentleness
Breathing passion into every part of the heart
Growing a simplicity that beckons for light
Which captures the truth in its brilliance

Our stories are different, yet
We each long for the laughter and praise
That leads us toward joy that stays
Alive through the end of each day
Leaves us sure that we have what it takes
To sigh in silence . . . breathlessly
Dreams which heal every pain
And spark a twinkle in the eyes of those
Who know that this love living within us
Is a love that brings true serenity

Our stories are different
Yet they remain the same
Tales of convictions that crave
The light that smiles through the heart
Piercing the darkness with assurance
Forcing all the worries from the thoughts
And reminding us why we have it all
If we have the One who gave us life
And continues to abide on the inside

Our stories are tales of thanks to Him
Who created us and gave us the opportunity
To share in His grace and His love
With faith that believes beyond the prayer
And promise that warrants all our best
Because we can know that we have the chance
To reach out and paint our world
In inspiration that comes from above
A wonder that comes from knowing the Son
Who was sent to us by a God who is LOVE

Freedom

Freedom to believe
The way my heart says to
Freedom to give
From the depths of my soul
Freedom to live
The way my God tells me to
Freedom to feel
Passionate and full of praises
For the One who created me
And gave His life so I might
Accompany Him in eternity!

Freedom, liberty to breath
Like light twinkling in the stars
Wind brushing the softest thoughts
Laughter coloring grace and hope
Freedom to express your faith
And freedom to remain silent
Both rejoice in the choice
That is honest and spontaneous
A phrase of sweetest abandon
Wrestling hope from its shell
Of fears and tears that cover
The years in darkness
That appears when sorrow and strife
Are allowed to shadow a heart
Fade a feeling of freedom
Into the night of a prison
Created on control's persuasion
Freedom opens the door to blessings
That are poured out on souls
Who know that God frees everyone
From their own prison
Of pain, sorrow and dejection

From the grief, worry and rejection
From the loss, dread – with protection
From all the past that haunts
With memories of sins who taunt

Freedom in Christ flows in the veins
Of those who know true freedom
Comes with a knowledge that salvation
Is a gift of grace through faith
Brought by our blessed Savior
To those who heed His still, small voice
Discovered in His Holy Word – the Bible

Thank God I'm free to hear Him speak!

Ephesians 2:8–9
King James Version

[8] For by grace are ye saved through faith; and that not of yourselves: it is the gift
of God:

[9] Not of works, lest any man should boast.

A Week of Prayer

Monday reminded me to give
God all the glory and praise
While I ask Him to please save
All the ones in need of His
Sweet mercy and grace

Tuesday I thought I would try
To give all my heart to kindness
Through a kind word or deed
According to God's will I'd heed
My heart's hope, faith and love

Wednesday taught me to grow
In wisdom, joy and assurance
That all my soul was an open door
For God to fill me up with inspiration
Free me from darkness with His light

Thursday I realized I needed to pray
Say some things I'd left unsaid
Words from the heart to reach Him
The One who gave me a second chance
To reach heaven's shore after a while

Friday showed me that my soul was alive
Filling up my being with pure joy with no strife
Revealing compassion that soothed my worries
Left me assured, without so many fears
Finally knowing that He was my promise

Saturday I wondered from hope to faith
Gathering my supplications and requests
Together with a feeling of graciousness

Gentling my struggles with life and living
Relieving all my doubts with sincere promises

Sunday was the day that I came away from
A service filled with a calming caress
From the hand that completes my life
With His boundless energy and love, lighting
My spirit from above, where my soul longs to go

Living on a prayer, my week is like a kaleidoscope
Of hope, faith and love – sent from God above
To assure me that I am a child of the King of Kings
The One who makes me smile and sing . . . psalms
Of joy unspeakable, love unbelievable, peace unfathomable

His love is a wonder inexplicable . . . Love unconditional!

If I were the color of love

If I were the color of darkness
Night blackening my vision
While my eyes twinkle gentle
Like the stars, drifting in song
Caressing the sky with tones
Of life beyond the blessings

If I were the color of laughter
Lighting the soul with joy
Elating the world with warmth
Vibrant and pure, feelings so true
They cry out with delight
Insight into the heart's beauty

If I were the color of storms
Rainbows pouring across the noon
After the rain has departed
Left only the music of pastel lines
To embrace the mind who sees
God's artwork flowing over the trees

If I were the color of silence
Serene and soulful as peaceful dreams
Faded into the smiles of kindness
Brought to the one who knows only
Prayers felt on the heart's shadows
Praising the Lord for His stillness

If I were the color of blessings
Sent on the wings of angel's breath
Shining on hopes and devotions
Reflecting on the simplicity of joy
That lingers on the touch of His hand
Reaching down to my spirit with a caress

If I were the color of love
I would sing to God above of the many
Miracles He's given me in this life
And thank Him for grace, faith and more . . .
The sense of purpose that comes from
Living for the Son who is so pure and so good!

Nourishment

Pouring down the pane, singing
It's the praise of soft rain
Gentle, like a sweet kiss falling
On whispering, hopeful lips

Gracious and gifted with faith
Painting the countryside in hues
Of misty gray music, forgiving
Thriving on the nourishment
It drenches with life, a pure diet
On black earth and vibrant petals
Caressing, like laughter
Dancing on the hope of a hereafter
When tears so timidly mingled
With showers of simplicity
Feelings of mystery, sensitive
To the breath of God sending us
Remedies to our worries, our doubts
Captured on the drops of belief
Sprinkling compassion through
Dreams and promises of a moment
When His love will pour out
A blessing more wholesome than
Any downpour from the heavens

Temple

Isn't it incredible
      That we can be the temple
Of the Holy Spirit
      Who brings a sense of assurance
Wisdom, hope, comfort
      Peace that is like a smile
Kind and bright
      As soothing as sunshine
Dewdrops or rainfall
      Pulsing against the ground
Almost as gently
      As His spirit whispers
Into silence and prayers
      Love that is unconditional
Life beyond this temple
      That is home to Him
The Holy Spirit
      Third person of the trinity
Gentling, gifting us
      With hope, faith and love
That comes from God above

Isn't it amazing? Isn't love like this
      Worthy of praising?
I worship Him in spirit and in truth
      Always remembering
He fills up my heart and soul
      With a love that can only grow
More pure, abundant and adoring
      Love like His is worth knowing!

You Are The Light

You shined your light into my thoughts
Illuminating hope and faith
Showing me the joy found in grace
Revealing the love abiding
With praise that comes from the heart
And prayers that free the soul
With kindness that lets me know
You are alive within my spirit

You lit up the shadows of my heart
With healing, revealing the worst
Clearing away the debris of doubt
And cleaning me in a way
That made me feel I should shout
With the wonder that came
When you emptied my spirit
Of all the darkness and damage

You flashed a brilliance into my depths
Revealing the need there
The anxiety and regret, the neglect
That had left me with a dreary
Lifeless sadness, gloomy emptiness
In need of your gentle compassion
The breath of your mercy
Reassuring and clarifying my yearnings

You washed my passions in hues
Of vibrant appreciation
Thanks for the many ways
You taught me to give my very best
With no thought for the gift

Only thinking of the glory that comes
From giving without expectation
Living without gratification

Loving without anticipation
For any true gift is meaningless
Without the promise
That the gift is as gracious
As a psalm for the one
Who is in need and should heed
God's plea for redemption
That comes from His free gift

You, sweet Jesus, are the way to see
Faith become a living, breathing
Belief that plants an everlasting seed
Into those souls who agree
God's word is the truth that assures
Love from above pours down
Into the hearts and souls who desire
To follow Him throughout all time

Just Take A Moment

Just take a moment and breathe
Listen to the silence
Reflect on a sweet dream
Laugh, smile, whisper into the light
Joys and freedoms, inspirations
That heal and fulfill

Just take a moment and breathe
Call out to the heavens
Ask God for grace and protection
Find a new direction
Encourage a heart to pray
Learn to rejoice in the present day

Just take a moment and breathe
Look to the azure skies
See all the glories God has painted
Along the mountains, coastlines, seas
Through the heart and soul
Into the blessings felt through eternity

Just take a moment and breathe
Lift up your eyes to believe
In the spirit's quest for purity and peace
Insights into faith that is a living thing
Lasting through the worries and sorrows
Reassuring there are good things in the tomorrows

Just take a moment and breathe
Sing a song of praise
Beckon to the grace that soothes and calms
Encourages the heart to take a chance
To risk the thought of losing
And anticipate the future

Just take a moment and breathe
Plant a seed in someone's heart
Share a psalm, a hope, a thought
Of gentle passions and pleasant ideas
All the love that reminds you to give
From the soul – the gift of kindness

I Am His

I am His
My Master
My friend
The One who
Will be there til the end

I am His
My light – my love
My guide – my truth
The One who gave life to
The Child who believes in Him

I am His
My Hope – My faith
My comfort – my grace
The One who gave me
Assurance of my fate

I am His
My kindness – my praise
My prayer for a better way
The One who saved me
And gave me hope of eternity

I am His
My joy – my peace
My miracle – my belief
The One who gave to me
The sweetest feeling of relief

I am His
My inspiration – my song
My life – my warmth

The One who knows my heart
The Maker – Creator – Father

I am His
My feelings of worthiness
My spirit of real life – always
The One who stirs my passion
Shows me the meaning of giving

I am His
My heart and soul
My satisfaction and knowing
That love is alive and growing
On the inside of those who know Him

Hues of Kindness

Indigo dreams smile through
Clouds of silvery light
Breathing silent whispers
Within prayers to the Creator
Who knows hearts and souls
And comforts through sweet hope

Cerulean stardust moments
Brighten lives with a dance of joy
Refreshing yearnings deep and sparkling
With reflections of kindness
Published upon a prayer, imploring
His will to fill a heart with affection
A mind with acceptance
A spirit with tender faith

Cobalt musings, echoing
Laughter into a life, soothing
Lifting and cheering, enlightening
The one who listens to the silence
Which brings a gentle kiss
To the naked sighs of insight
Inspiration alive and thriving
Igniting fires of passion that plead
For brilliant rays of precious grace
Sewn together with fibers
Of love and longing
Feelings, promises of pleasure
Tantalizing and wistful

Azure skies calm the fears
Of those who feel the quiet
That awakens the soul to a song
A psalm of lovely, lingering ardor

Tenderness that trembles
With sensitivity and charm
Adoration for the One who knows
All that lives inside a heart

Sapphire tones of secret flavors
Spicy and salty as tears
Seasoning the thoughts, bold and full
Of memories, reveries, ambitions
All the things that make up a life
And make a life worthwhile
A life God can use is a life that knows
Giving is greater than gaining anything

Shine your light – let it glow, glittering
As alive to the old as the young
Dazzling the eye who beholds such a shine
Amid the gleaming, luminous blush
Of a delicate heart who knows the soul
In God's hands is a soul who can rest
Assured, certain, knowing
There is tranquility and harmony
Beyond this earthly home

There in the lazuline heavens
Is a home that is more beautiful
Than any words or music
More alive than any color or creation
More vivid than any array of flowers
And more brilliant than any poem
Can portray, thought praise
Or reflection grasp

Someday, I am going there – to that heavenly home
And when I meet the One who gave me life
I know that there will be more love than I've ever known
I'm so thankful for the promise of paradise

I'm so thankful for the Light that is shining inside
Reminding me that He is alive, a fire who inspires
My heart, my soul, my mind, my spirit
He is forever there with me, eternally fulfilling
With love that is beyond any description

He is wonder of wonders – eternal peace
Sweet rose of Sharon . . . pure freedom
He is my King, Prince of Peace, the only answer
To my longing for a better way, a higher truth
A sense of awareness that God is still there
Abiding in glory, alive and granting answers
To all those prayers that we're still breathing
On the wind, in the whispers of gentle grace,
Along the heart that praises with faith

God is alive and He is always willing to listen
To any prayer that reveals a heart, a spirit
The inkling that He is still humbly worshiped
With respect and love – true adoration for Him
The One who gives each one the gift of grace
And faith that warms the soul with soothing
Joy that lives because His love is alive in the heart

Summer Sun

He breathes hues of light
Into the dark shadows
Kissing dewdrops
With warming laughter
Hugging lively petals
With gentle glimmers

He whispers joy into the spirit
Sighs a caress across naked skin
Enlightening and enlivening
Thrilling the spirit with passionate
Promises of a new dawn
A tangerine sun, bathing
Darkness with a vibrant smile

He heats the moments in hues
Of robin's egg blue and blushing rose
Lavender, lilac and happiness
Thriving on the afternoon, awakening
Twilight to the colors of a new moon
Lifting spirits and writing beautiful
Poetry across the frosty night

He is a vow of longing
In the song that echoes
On the wind and sings blessings
Through the prayers that reflect
A inner healing, a willingness
To know gratitude within the soul
And grace that praises the One
Who created the summer sun

Prayers and Psalms

I utter a prayer
I gasp a psalm

Soft, tender kisses
A gentle embrace
Soothing beyond description
My heart will race
Trying to catch up
With the love flowing
Through his veins

A whisper of joy
Stirring my hopes
With passion and promises
Of lights in hues of
Lavender and lilac
Underneath a tangerine
Moon glowing with truth
Bright and vibrant
Inspiration, inner beauty

A sigh of God's light
Murmur of insight
Through a heart alive
With a sense of serenity
That stirs light in those
Who know love so sure
Love that lasts
Love that is kind, alive
Spoken of in prayers
That I Breathe into God's ear

With him, I am myself

Creative Thoughts

Give a thought from the depths of your heart
A kindness, a twinkling — of laughter and dreams
A light that embraces with wonder and serenity
A imagination filled with so many good things

Give help and healing — honest faith and strength
Capable of encouraging, lifting the heaviest anxiety
With miraculous blessings — surrounded by inspiration
Sent on flames of love, kissing the soul with feelings
Meant to capture hearts in a warm and graceful sigh

With your words and reflections, captivate and assure
Remind a heart it's loved and fill dreams with liberty
To be whispered on a song coloring life in hues of light
Music breathing gentleness through the heart and soul

Whisper exhilaration that flows through crimson veins
In poetry and prose, rhythms of blessings and reveries
Shine love across the empty page, with nouns and verbs
Delight the spirit who reads and finds fulfillment here
Soothe a soul who is in need of your depiction of faith

Give with your mind, your heart, your soul – your whole
Sparkle life through your ink – creativity on your page, God's grace!

Where Can I Go?

If there ever comes a prayer
When He's no longer there
Where will I go?

If there ever comes a plea
When He fails to listen to me
Where will I go?

If there ever comes a night
That my heart is filled with fright
Where will I go?

Where can I go – only to Him
The One who saved my soul
And is there to make me whole
He is the only place I can find
To hide my thoughts when I'm lost
To heal my faith when I doubt
To guide me home when I'm down
To share my dreams, my needs, my beliefs
And know that He will always give
The best advice, comfort, counsel
He will always reassure me, cure me
Feed my faith with amazing grace
If there ever comes a time
When I have lost all my hope
Where will I go?

If there ever comes a day
When I hurt too much to just pray
Where will I go?

If there ever comes a friend
Who turns out to be a enemy
Where will I go?

Where can I go – only to Jesus
The One who forgives my sins
Helps me to begin again
Fills me with faith that lives
And dries up all my tears

Where can I go? Only to Him
The One who makes a way
Where there seems to be no way
The One who fills me with love
When I feel sure I'm totally numb
The One who leads me toward home
When I have lost all control

Where can I go? Only to Jesus
He is always there to take away the fear
Filling me up with joy, peace and hope
Leaving me sure I know the way to love
Is felt inside a heart that is under His blood

Where can I go?
If not to Him . . . I have no hope
If not to Him . . . I have no way
If not to Him . . . I have no peace
If not to Him . . . I have no salvation
If not to Him . . . I have no life worth saving

Where can I go?
Only to Jesus – my hope, faith and comfort
The One sent from up above
To assure me God is Love

Eternally Mine

There were tears, salty and silent
Combing a path down my face
In rivers of longing, hopeless and desperate
Miserable and as dark as dusk's heavy pace
Never allowing a piece of light to glimmer
Through the shadows of dread
Darkening the depths of my spirit
Soulless and soundless like the tears
Clinging to my lashes, a whisper
Kissing the fate of my yearning heart
As it fades and falls away from
The screaming inside my forlorn thoughts

There were prayers, feebly prayed
Self-pity painting lonely, abandoned visions
Through my thirsty pores, penetrating
Sounds of grace and goodness with weak stabs
That remind me still of the aching shame
The shadows, sullen and wan, sorrowful
Sending horrific doubts and apprehension
Into the light that had once been a part of me
But now was easily the flicker beneath
Eclipsed kindness and compassion
Gasping out pain that would never be forgiven
For invading my laughter, my smile
With grizzled gray rainfall that taught me
To listen to the sound of the shower
And know that this wasn't the tears of God
The way someone once told me
This was nurturing, sustenance, nourishment
Sent to fill the earth with miracles

My tears were briny and sweet sounding trinkets
Of breathless prayers, faded faith
Feelings that had left me sure I couldn't possibly
Find the beauty and joy and hope
That had once been a part of me, the heart of me
Gentling the worries and struggles with a promise
Of light, laughter, love that would fill me up
To the brink of overflowing onto a cold world
Warming the flames of kindness and joy
With a beautiful faith that is overflowing
The pace of that blood sucking enemy
Who hides within black sin and iniquity

It would take prayers, deep, moving prayers,
Prayers of faith, feeling and grace that lifts the spirit
To whisper through my beliefs, into my sensitivities
Where God could finally relieve me of the chains
The pain and blazing flame of wretched anguish
Coloring my heart in faded shades of gray

Now, I feel a thrill and the feeling is real
Light shimmers across my heart, my thoughts
Beckoning me to listen to the hope drawing me in
Like a long lost friend, raining peace across my soul
Wisdom into my thoughts and a glow of compassion
Through the depths of my spirit – joy unspeakable
Shines across my life, filling the holes that once stood
Empty and yawning, yearning for a sense of truth
To fill up my life with kindness, faith and real love
Love like this is so amazing that it is almost a song
To simply speak of its hues of tangerine suns
Sparkling stardust and moonbeams that brighten
The world who whispers light across my life

With a gentle hand, God raised me up to abide in the high
That is alive in the gifts of His faith, hope and love
Now, I don't cry stinging tears – I cry joy filled tears
Tears of love, light and life that lives on the inside
Where God's spirit has come to reside – eternally mine!

Do You Feel?

Some people feel the rain, others just get wet — bob marley

Do you feel
The hue of April
Whispering through the spirit?

Do you feel
The breath of Autumn
Coloring the world in hues of passion?

Do you feel
The lingering laughter
In a sunrise at the sea?

Do you feel
The music of a song
Creating such intimacy?

Do you feel
The joy of a child
Caressing a puppy's fleece?

Do you feel
The angel that is alive
In the heart and soul?

Do you feel
The miracle of life
Piercing through crimson veins?

Do you feel
The rain falling
Melting the dustcloud?

Do you feel, my friend
Do you feel it all
The happiness and sadness
The winter, spring and fall?
Do you feel the silence
The echo of a hope
The prayer breathed on a moment
Sincere faith – sweet love?

Do you feel, my friend
Do you feel?

Magic

The world is full of magic things, patiently
waiting for our senses to grow sharper

W.B. YEATS

There is magic in the twinkling eyes
Of a small, innocent child who smiles
There is magic in the laugh of delight
In a heart who sees a wonderous birth
There is magic in the light of a word
Focused on kindness instead of being heard

There is magic in the new dawn, the star
The feeling that races through a tender heart
Who knows about giving without expectation
Living without gratification,
Feeling without awakening
A need for recompence

There is magic – in hopes and dreams
In faith and all the little things
In wonders that melt away the sorrow
And remind us all that there is grace for tomorrow

There is magic – in the caress of a smile
Given by someone who blesses a heart
With inspiration, kindness, acceptance
All the love that brings assurance and affection

There is magic – in the soul who knows faith
Whispers a prayer and lingers in grace
Knows God is alive, filling up the inside
Of one who listens to His gentle spirit

There is magic – in psalms and praise
In new life that comes with salvation
In freedom from all those things that bring pain
In feeling alive to the new moment, the new way
The new joy that abides in the one who prays

There is magic – in the sun and rain
In the dewdrop and the gentle rose
In the light of the stardust night
And the miracle of one shooting out of sight

There is magic – in love
That is alive and thriving, striving to give more
Than it receives, with a open heart and sincere spirit
Love that is scented with a blushing aroma of insight
Inspiration and music created from the joy inside

There is magic – from the brilliance of a heart
Who knows that real love comes from God's thought
Of giving away a breath of life to the one who listens
To the gentle, teasing urging of a feeling of expectation

Love like this is the beginning of true living!

A Heavenly Home

Fear of the unknown is a living fear, igniting a disquiet within the
soul who is uncertain of its home in the hereafter . . . calm your
soul with a whisper of His amazing grace poured across your mind,
leaving hope sublime

QUOTE BY POET

We fear the new, the untried, the untested
We fear pain, angst, destruction
We fear God, the devil, death
We fear loss, lasting distress
We fear hell, where there is no rest
That awful place where God's grace
Is never felt and love has left us
With only unbearable pain

There is a way to leave the fear behind
Experience true peace
Within the soul and mind
Know that in the afterlife
There will be sweetest joy and peace
A love that is overflowing
With amazing grace
A light that resembles faith
Beckons us to become a part of the family
Who God will take home one day
To live forever, eternally
There in heaven

The way has been paved
By nail scarred hands
The price will never cost us

More than a simple prayer
Of repentance . . . simply ask forgiveness
And God's grace will take you in
To always know this friend
Who will be with you til the very end

Listen to your heart
He sacrificed it all
You only need to have faith
And He will pay your way
Into that wonderful place
Where we abide eternally
In the light – the love
That is God from above
Comforting, calming, coloring
The entire air – with a joyful way
Of knowing a better day

He has paved the way
You simply step out in faith
And answer the call to be saved
From death, pain and the grave
A Heavenly home awaits
Our last thoughts are truly tranquil
Because we know in our hearts
We have every right to be thankful

His Beloved Children

Vibrant tangerine sunset
Rests high on the azure skies
Freeing thoughts with spontaneity
Alive within silences cry
Soothing, warm and brilliant
Rhyming with the robin's chirping
Melody glowing on gossamer wings
Of butterfly's new beginning

Breathtaking light of the autumn
Painting the landscape in dreams
Of dazzling hopes and promises
Creating a earth caught up by psalms
Laughing praises that linger and charm
Every thought with a caress, a smile
Of love and joy, worship of God
Who knows these moments are blessings
Sent down from the splendors of heaven
Where grace and glory adore
With feelings as sweet and serene
As poetry being sung to the moon
Glowing and glimmering with twinkling
Stardust quivers, sapphire whispers
Gentle embraces from the mystery
That is His pleasure to give us
His children, who learn to cherish Him more
With these reminders that we're eternally loved

Listen

Listen to the heart who knows how to pray
With faith, hope and love that will not dismay.

Listen to the spirit who knows to wait
Pausing to praise the God who did create

Listen to the whisper of His sweet grace
Painting hearts in hues of a kind embrace

Listen to the joy in a child's laughter
Promising bliss lives in the hereafter

Listen to the music that calms the rain
With comforting hope that slays every pain

Listen to the breath abiding inside
Purring serenity that does reside

Listen to the dance that is like a fire
Shadowing the world with life I admire

Listen to the dream of an aching psalm
Gazing at the stars who apply a balm

Listen to the light who sends gentle rays
Covering hopes with grace that does amaze

Listen to the passion that feeds the soul
Igniting sparks of love to make you whole

Breathe

Breathe grace against
A tangerine moon who lights
The depths of the heart

Breathe passion across
A scarlet rose who grows
Through rain and jewels of dew

Breathe faith along
A sapphire sky who vibrates
With nightfall's sweet silence

Breathe laughter into
A lemonade hue of summer who
Smiles with overwhelming joy

Breathe light around
A lavender glow of kindness
Giving tender gifts of guidance

Breathe promises over
A silvery whisper of prayer
Sharing blessings from the soul

Breathe love through
A burgundy sigh of compassion
Delivering hope that is everlasting

Simplicity

Dewdrops sliding down
A soft, bright petal
Nurturing and gentle
Like a loving teardrop
Embracing my thoughts

The whispering breeze
Calling a heart as it passes
Murmurs a psalm on the
Sunlit morning of a summer
Day filled with joyful promise

Starlight falling lightly
On a silent, moonlit night
As a ghostly song lingers
On the edge of darkness
Calling to the fireflies in June

Tangerine sunshine warming
Naked thoughts and reassuring
My hope of laughing colors
In hues of amber, gold and crimson
Embracing my heart with a poem

Radiant blushing roses gracing
A garden of my soul's dreams
Inspiring me to touch the foliage
With faithful, warm tenderness
Reflecting all my best emotions

Serenity that welcomes me into
A sweet sincere prayer to the creator
Of all this mystery we share as
Blessings from a loving and giving

God who listens to our true plea

Rain showers that bring flavors of
Breathless inspiration and insight
To season my heart with enlightenment
Easy smiles and kindness that brings
A healing and hope on the inside

Music that rests on the soul, speaking
To the silence with wise, warm words
Filled with thanksgiving and purpose
Peace that leaves the spirit alive
With compassionate joy overflowing

A twinkle in the tender eyes of one
Who is willing to live, love and give
From the depths of the heart
Kindness and grace, faith that weaves
Threads of light into spiritual awakening

A little hand, so small and trusting
Placed into my own with a knowing
That I will lead them across a road
Or in the direction of safety and hope
That is as secure and sure as the dawn

Sighs soothing as the milky clouds
Drifting on cerulean with miracles
Meeting of breath and moist air
Praising the way that awakens
The soul to this dance of the spirit

Mornings with a hungry thought
Feelings that reveal a heart
Simple ways to embrace a soul
With thanksgiving, blessings
Alive on the life filled with love

Dandelions

One hand reaches
Out to pluck a buttery
Yellow blossom
This eye sees the beauty
Softening my petal

Another hand grasps
My heart with intentions
Of loosening my roots
Plucking me from
The cool dark earth
This eye sees only the ugly
Hues veining through me, a weed
Needing to be retrieved
From the soil I desperately need

Still another hand reaches
Out to me, welcoming
My fertility – breathing
Exhaling enthusiasm
Releasing my precious seed
To the world who pleads
With me to write my poetry
In the soft warm breeze

Yes, I promise the truth
Is that beauty certainly
Is in the eye of the
Beholder, weather they're
A child at heart or
A gardener with hope
Or a writer of breathtaking
Thanks to God

Tell me who do you say that I am?

He is my almighty, my always, my armor
He is my blessing, my breath, my boldness
He is my comfort, my carpenter, my compassion
He is my divinity, my devotion, my delight
He is my earth, my eternity, my enlightenment
He is my faith, my fulfillment, my future
He is my God, my gift, my grace
He is my hope, my heart, my heaven
He is my insight, my inspiration, my inner guide
He is my joy, my judgement, my Jesus
He is my king, my kindness, my keeper
He is my light, my love, my laughter
He is my maker, my music, my morning
He is my necessity, my nurturer, my night
He is my openness, my oil, my offering
He is my purity, my praise, my peace
He is my quest, my quiet, my quivering
He is my rock, my redeemer, my rest
He is my shepherd, my sight, my sensitivity
He is my truth, my treasure, my theology
He is my understanding, my unity, my usefulness
He is my value, my vastness, my virtue
He is my worth, my warmth, my wisdom
He is my xenia, my xenas, my xenodochy
He is my yearning, my yore, my yesterday
He is my zeal, my zenith, my zest

He is my Jesus, He is my God, He is my Holy Spirit
He is the One I love . . . He is my everything
Yesterday, tomorrow and today – always
He holds the key to death and the grave
As well as my eternity – Praise His holy name!

Matthew 16:13–19

King James Version

[13] When Jesus came into the coasts of Caesarea Philippi, he asked his disciples, saying, Whom do men say that I the Son of man am?

[14] And they said, Some say that thou art John the Baptist: some, Elias; and others, Jeremias, or one of the prophets.

[15] He saith unto them, But whom say ye that I am?

[16] And Simon Peter answered and said, Thou art the Christ, the Son of the living God.

[17] And Jesus answered and said unto him, Blessed art thou, Simon Barjona: for flesh and blood hath not revealed it unto thee, but my Father which is in heaven.

[18] And I say also unto thee, That thou art Peter, and upon this rock I will build my church; and the gates of hell shall not prevail against it.

[19] And I will give unto thee the keys of the kingdom of heaven: and whatsoever thou shalt bind on earth shall be bound in heaven: and whatsoever thou shalt loose on earth shall be loosed in heaven.

In the Dark

Dark as the sky who
Publishes stars
Reflecting the dance
Against a tangerine
Moon, longing for
Dawn and truth

Dark as the circles
Underneath sunken eyes
Who only see
Insomnia's gloom
Coloring the night
In melancholy and dread
For moments of sleepless
Fists raised toward angst

Dark as the black
Cat who is haunted
By the shadow
Of superstition
Saying bad luck follows
One who sees it
Crossing their path

Dark as the fate
Of a lonely song
Drifting through the
Soul of one who
Knows despair — grief
And the grace that
Caresses the naked
Thoughts of a heart
Who releases

It's dread to the
Lavender light
Of dawn

Dark as the forest
That breaths
Shallow breaths
Through dead branches
Of oak and pine
Leaves lost to earth
Where decay
Will offer grief-stricken
Pain to the waves
Of debris in hues of
Graying grim gorges

Dark as the pain
Winding it's way through
Crimson veins
Filled with flowing
Antibiotics called love
Who hope to heal
The illness
Of greed, hate, shame

Dark as death
In its blackest
Cape of captivity
Covering the soul in
Misery and mystery
Mourning for music
That bleeds hope
Into the emotions

Dark as eyes
Twinkling
Delight from a place
Of inspiration
And insight
Into the gentle beauty
Of warm, wistful
Wishes

Dark caresses hearts
With clouds
Of reassuring prayers
Prayed with thanksgiving
For the waking moments
When rays of sunlight
Break through the
Doubtful darkness
In blooms of laughter
Brilliant and vibrant
As the light that lives
In the heart love fills

Praying

Praying from the heart
Whispered thoughts, yearnings
Breathed into the sanctuary
Or the pillow or the ear
Of one who will listen to your
Hopeful prayer

Praying from the lips
Naked beliefs, feelings
Bright as crimson that pours
From the veins of the One
Who gave us a chance
To be reborn

Praying from the silence
That glimmers on stardust
Arrayed in brilliant gladness
Exhilaration flowing like rainfall
Against a soft cheek, teary
From elated faith

Praying from the grace
That colors souls in hues of light
Soft and gentle, like a caress
Of inspiration and compassion
Dancing with laughter
From a joyful thought

Praying from the plans
Of a spirit that understands
Psalms of thanksgiving and peace
Come to life on the conviction
Of those who choose to listen
To the Spirit's direction

Praying from the insight
Of a holy, healing hope
Kindness overflows in rich floods
Of beauty, brilliance and goodness
That comes from heeding
The answers He bestows

Praying from the spirit
With tender assurance you're giving
All your best, your hope and faith
The love that you possess
Because He blessed you with
Love that is fully alive!

On the inside, you can know
Your prayer is touching God's spirit
And you can be certain that He is willing
To answer those prayers you're contemplating
With the promise of a heavenly guide
Who is always by your side!

The Holy Spirit is always
Making intercession for us

Luke 11:13
If ye then, being evil, know how to give good gifts unto your children: how much more shall your heavenly Father give the Holy Spirit to them that ask him?

Blue

The color of skies
Enchanting the mind
As it whispers azure promises
Taking flight with wings
So feathery swift
Like a gentle flame
Creating the fire that burns
Within one who sees
Only good within the spirit
Who listens to God

The color of laughter
Soothing and soft
Breathing music that echoes
On the hope of the heart
Who listens to the rhythm
Of senses so calm and sweet
They leave dewdrop dreams
Swimming in tears of peace
Where joy has been seen
Drifting downstream

The color of silence
Caressing naked thoughts
With whimsical, passive calm
That welcomes brilliant desires
To reach beyond the want
To the soul of the thought
Where only inspiration can thrive
Surviving the dreary tides
Of times that bring dread
Fear and disillusionment
A sense of despair that wrecks
The heart who is filled with

Wishes for tomorrow's thrill

The color of truth
Abiding in the kindness
That reminds us to live
With prayers sent to heaven
On wings of psalms that smile
Upon the angel's song
Caressing the soft charms
Of One who knows our hearts
Loves us through the sorrow
And guides us into tomorrow
Where we will discover the way
To worship and pray
With a faith that was raised
With Jesus this Easter

The color of grace
Powerful and praising
Making a way for the spirit
To feel assured of it's ability
To answer from the heart
That God has given a gift
Abiding within the one
Who listens to the sound
Of His unconditional love
As it makes a way for us
To be saved to the uttermost

Ephesians 2:8–9
King James Version
[8] For by grace are ye saved through faith; and that not of yourselves: it is the gift
of God: [9] Not of works, lest any man should boast.

My Everything

Laughing, dancing, singing
With joy beyond imagining
Oaks, birch and emerald pines
Caress my soul with gentle thoughts
Beautiful whispers that soothe
And brighten my heart's solitude

Silent, yet breathing sighs of pleasure
Awakening naked embraces of light
As it shades the sun's brilliant fires
With the faded touch of wind's breath
As it falls across the meadow and hill
Capturing the scene during Autumn's chill

Loving, like a tender kiss filled with passion
Wistful and rich beyond any enthusiasm
Lasting through the night's starry reflections
Moonbeams and twinkling so vast that they
Illuminate the heavens with kindness so sure
It comforts the broken heart and wearysoul

Fauna so mysterious it echoes with caution
Of feelings rare and genuine, like light
Shimmering across the still waters and seas
Creating a rhythm so sweet it keeps the mind
Promised empathy alive within the spirit
Securing hope that lives deeper than the fishes

Beauty that soars across the dawn
In hues of faith and serenity, shades
So deep they fade into the attire of sunshine
Light so vivid and wonderful it will seem
Like it can edge forever with their parade
Of carefully frosted, blushing blossoms

Rejoicing, praising, praying
Like thoughts of the Son and Savior
Melodious and graceful, pure as chastity
Life reflects the innocence of One
Who knows the heart, the soul, the hope
That lives inside those who abide faithfully
To the Son who shines brighter than the sun!

He is the light that is alive, a fire
On the inside, where He lives, fulfills
Gives the answers and heals
All the worries and fears and tears
Assuring the heart that He is always near
Protecting, promising, pledging to be
The One who gives hearts the chance they need

To believe, achieve and conceive
Of a hope that lives eternally

Jesus is my everything!

Shadows

Shadows of clouds fall across the sunlit moment, breaking through
dawn like a peace filled thought whispers music into a heart
QUOTE BY POET

Lovely shadows
Dark and wise
Drift across skies
Lit up in morning glow
Intense as a new fallen snow
Alive with bleached insights
Into the peaceful calm
Of a gentle dawn

Secretive shadows
Edging the light of day
With mystery and charm
A welcome from the stars
Who are being erased
By laughing sunlight rays
In hues of lavender praise
Wandering across the vista
Of a luscious, blushing sight

Brilliant sparks of joy
Filled shadows, the muse
Lift the night's echoing
Voice of vibrant visions
Captivating, soothing and sensing
A reality beyond the norm
Wise, wild and worn
By seas that are wind blown

And shores that adorn
Lively flavors of pleasure
Sent to the heavens
On waves of purity shown
On the edges of soft
And succulent flow
Which welcomes the traveler
Home to the oceanic sea
Of beauty, thrills and dreams

Clouds drift soundlessly
Through shadows
In silent reverie
Across the still, clear sky
Breathing out blessings
As they pass by
Luscious feelings animating
The passage of stars as
They twinkle to a close
On the night that has come
And gone, blinking lazily
As a dream passes across
The dark and soft hues
Of lilac charm races to the
Heavens on prayers
Of praise that penetrate
The very soul

The shadows shade
A dazzling sun as it gleams
Across the morning
Alive and creating warmth
To bath the rose
Melting the dew and
Healing the heart who
Feels lost on the earth
And longs for the sweet

Thrill of heaven, paradise
Where the exhilaration
Ecstasy – will blaze and flame
Lighting up the moments
In adoring grace that lifts
Hearts and souls, colors worlds
In sparks of serenity that welcomes
Our souls into the rich, brilliant
Peace of everlasting love

Shadows detail the ways
Our hearts will be amazed
By God's embrace
When we reach that place
Of unending joy and love
With One who releases
Every soul from its pain
Wipes every tear away
And leaves the heart
Filled with love that dances
To music played by angels

Shadows have a way of enhancing
Faith in hearts who are open
To knowing love that is accepting
Of even the ones who need direction

Shadows are there to teach us
To listen to the soft, sweet whispers
That come beneath the clouds
On dawns who are alive with belief

Shadows remind us to appreciate
The deep and brilliant peace
That is left on the edges of hopes
Who leave us feeling like we're dreaming

Shadows tell the sun to soften the light
That sends assurance of love across the night

God is Alive

Silence paints even the shadows in hues of serenity and soft song
that leaves the soul sure of grace that abides on heartfelt psalms

BY POET

With a gentle whisper, kissing naked skin
In laughter and soothing intimacy
Joy fades into the tangerine sunset
Melting away all pain and regret
Leaving only assurance that serenity
Paints notes of love across the lavender light
Of an evening prayer and promise
To the One who knows the depths of the heart
And leaves the soul trusting faith's word

Verses of love, hope and faith
Touch the thoughts with affection and grace
Pure praise poured out on the Father
Who welcomes His child into the heart to heart
With a voice that calms, sooths and confirms
That His love is a living thing – like the wind
It breathes harmony into the hereafter
Quieting every worry and anxiety
With perfect silence, flowing over with
Pure, sweet devotion and adoration
Exaltation of the One who is alive on the inside
An all-consuming fire who exhales light
And inspires the heart to cry
Tears of blessing and glory
Warmth in the soul who knows
God is Alive!

It Is Surely Wonderful

It is surely wonderful . . .
  To be found
In the parlors or diners
  At the water's edge
Along the beach or river
  Where there are blessings
Foaming from the shores

It is surely wonderful . . .
  To find a passion
Thriving with warmth
  Welcoming joys
Inspirations so alive
  They dance across
The moonlit night of autumn

It is surely wonderful . . . .
  To succeed at a dream
That blazes hot inside
  The soul who longs to
Arrive at the labyrinth
  Of change and colors
So rich and vibrant they breathe

It is surely wonderful . . .
  To awake to fresh laughter
Caressing the stars, the sun
  In whispers of compassion
Like grace in a psalm
  Prayers echo through the sky
On a faith that is so alive

It is surely wonderful . . .
       To know God is inside
The heart and soul
       Touching the naked mind
With pure peace and love
       That echoes faith along
The shadows beneath a full sun

It is surely wonderful . . .
       To believe the answers
Will always come
       Revealed in a way that
Only truth can portray
       With sincerity and praise
For the One who loves unconditionally

It is surely wonderful . . .
       To break free of grief
And know the joy within
       That pleads for serenity
Captures the promise of
       Beauty that feels so free
It blesses even the worst sinner

It is surely wonderful . . .
       To know the way to giving
A part of the heart and soul
       Living within the spirit
Increasing joy and hope
       Raises the sweetest glow
To caress the summer with love

It is surely wonderful . . .
       To paint the world in twinkling
Stars and milky moonbeams
       That drift across the night

Sending stirrings of intimacy
        Silent familiarity with the
Flavors of God's brilliant, amazing thoughts

It is surely wonderful . . .
        To know the One
Who created the sun
        Gentled the heart
Shaped the stars
        Twisted the laurel
Gave breath to us all

It is surely wonderful . . .
It is surely wonderful!

Beginning the Day

The best way to begin again
As the morning sun beams
Softly across the heart

Is to whisper a prayer of thanks
For all that you've been blessed with
Today and every day

Through joy and pain, happy or sad
You've known hope and faith
And an amazing, overwhelming love

The best way to start the day
Is to listen to your heart
And take a moment to pray

Thanking God for all that you are
All that you've been given
And all the light you've been shown

Thanking God for the breath in your lungs
The whisper of a smile on your lips
The gentle faith that keeps you believing

Thanking God for today and tomorrow
For the memories that are with you
Allowing you to appreciate all that you've seen

Thanking God for it all, whatever comes
Know that He will comfort and calm
With grace that fills your up your heart

The best way to begin a new day
As the sun warms your skin
Is to pray and praise with love
That keeps you giving your best!

A Clean Heart

Happiness is in the quiet, ordinary things — a table, a chair, a book
... and the petal falling from the rose, and the light flickering as we
sit silent.

—VIRGINIA WOOLF

Breathing in the silent thoughts
Of rich, green pasture
Maples and birch
Birthed on the tail end
Of a rain shower
In spring

Whispering in the dreams
Of colors in hues
Of lavender and lilac
Promises rich
Dancing light and love
Laughter from above
On the heart of one who knows
God is alive

Soothing the heart and soul
With beauty discovered
On winds and vibrant hugs
From the stardust night
As it flickers and smiles
Bidding souls delight
In psalms and prayers

Twisting and turning
Through rays of sunlight
As it embraces naked minds
With delicious inspirations
Feelings so sweet
Compassion swells within
Warming the heart
As well as the spirit
Comforting as
Music

Little things come to life
In the eyes of a child
Who loves so innocently
Purity dripping from the heavens
On milky clouds
So soft and kind they
Deny the thunder
Has ever roared in a storm
As they caress the skies
With simple hope

Create in me a clean heart
O God . . . create in me a right spirit
One who knows your love
And the answers
That come from above
With faith and assurance
That your love
Will give me all I need
Today, tomorrow, forever
Throughout eternity

In A Jar

In a jar of hope
Where joy and happiness
Are planted and grow
To maturity titled contentment
There I left my sorrows and grief
And all the little things
That have caused my heart to bleed
Disillusion, despair, discouragement

In a jar of faith
Where grace and mercy sweeten
My life with inspiration and prayers
Woven through layers of kindness
Where all my time has been spent
Giving and growing and being
Grateful for this journey
Which is taking me on to glory

In a jar of love
Where laughter lifts the spirit
Teaching me to believe
In the music of breathless dreams
Which carry me through the thoughts
That beckon me to create
From the sweetness of my heart
Complete compassion and praise

In a jar of miracles
Given by the Creator I love
I find gentleness and benevolence
Built on the poetry of psalms
So wise and sure and alive

They dance through my soul
Assuring me that I can know
God is with me through it all

I love the One who holds my heart and soul
In the center of His palm
Where I can always be sure
There is complete love and calm
Beauty beyond any song
Feelings that erase all the bad days
And keep me filled with adoration
For the One who breathes life into me

Agape

"... one can never leave home ... one carries the shadows, the
dreams, the dragons of home under one's skin, at the extreme
corners of one's eyes."

MAYA ANGELOU, LETTER TO MY DAUGHTER, 2008

Healing all my hidden hurts
With music, laughter and light
Sensations of silent winds
Blowing a caress against naked skin

Whispering joy through my heart
On wings of azure promises
Whistling, singing and dancing
Reflecting all the imaginings
Of a soul who bleeds warm hope
And melts through prayers
Of quiet truth, awakening silence
In bright, brilliant visions
Of inspiration, a muse so alive
It feels like the color of praise
Scarlet red, birthed in lavender
Wishing for touches of tangerine
Amber and gold and miracles so bold
They birth beauty in their path

Home is where the heart is, I've heard
And listened to the speaker with hope
Because I know my heart is in love
With the twinkling eyes that look into me
Welcome me and pleasure me
Break me away from the sorrow and fear
That causes me to wish I could always be

88

Where these eyes fill me up with courage
And make me alive in a way I've never been
Alive to the moment, passionate
Pure and praising the One who blesses
With a feeling so precious it embraces me
With joy I couldn't possibly express

I can only feel it – It's real and it's warm
And it caresses my very soul – It is home
Where the heart is . . . with eyes gentled by life
Reflecting my hope and faith and grace
And all the love I have to give

Home is where the heart is and my heart
Is with this man of my gratefulness
This man of my longing and laughing
Like light shining across my thoughts and a
Brilliant array of prayers so thankful
They are lifted up to the heavens
On hands who held their treasures with
A faith that abides in amazement
That He is blessing so richly, so kindly
With blessings that fold hands into praise
And lift heavy hearts to sing in a way
That can only be accepted as adoration
Worship of the One who created me
Gave me the courage to break free of pain
And love beyond my wildest imaginings
With faith, hope and peace that assures me
My heart belongs to a home of eternity

Love like this is beyond words
It's bigger than awesome and wilder
Than the night . . . it is growing fuller
With each passing expression of gentleness
That breathes a prayer up to Him

The One who is home to the love that
Has become agape, eternal, beyond measure

Love like this is the home I so treasure!

His Muse

In the still, cool silence
Of a summer's evening
I lift my eyes to the skies
And see the moon reflecting
All my thoughts and cares
As the stars twinkle, laughing
Like a caress to my soul

In the gentle kindness
Of a summer's softly lit night
There is a echo of hope
Drifting on the edge of my
Thoughts, creating tones
Of crimson whispers
At the heart of my poem

In the quiet joys of a moment
That radiates with breaths
Of light and inspiration, tender
As the pale rays that drift
Calming the nocturnal blows
Of wind, so feathery agile
Like a sigh against a silent tear

In the hues of ebony darkness
Waves of compassion, bright
Sympathetic to the blackness
That murmurs like a brook
Calming, resting in a faith
More honest and true
Than any dream could trace

In the night's contemplations
Peaceful caresses touch

Upon blessings so warm and rich
They flame like the passion
That rises on the inside of a heart
Who knows what it is to love
With all the feeling alive, assured

In the mystery of a vision
Rising high, like a bird on wing
Wishing and flowing and dreaming
Of all the colors and creations
God has blessed all our emotions
With . . . here in the moment
We can appreciate the brilliance

Radiating across the soul – His muse

Coloring My World

Passionate purple and scarlet vibrate
Through my veins, dancing light
Across my spirit, warm and bright
Like a healing hand, caressing my soul
With hope, faith and love that quiet fear

Dazzling lavender and tangerine promises
Whisper joy through me with laughing
Arrays of tender blossoms, dressed in prayers
That praise the creator for all this beauty
This wonderful grace and glory in floras

Festive rays of lemony sunshine beckon to me
Through the lively, vigorous contentment
Which blesses my emotions with dewy tears
Easing my sorrows and encouraging me to
Begin again, find a new dawn and happy thoughts

Pure innocence breathes a clean, snowy flow
Of winter's touch through my frosty reflections
Clear white restoration throbs in my heart
And I feel the virtue of an appeal to heaven weaving
Blessings, worship and glory into my thoughts

Silent turquoise, tinted with a soft sapphire applause
Sighs along my beliefs, thrilling and releasing peace
That delights in my soul song, singing breathlessly
Echoing devotion through me with inspirational calm
That awakens my dreams to believe in their grace

Moonbeams colored in hues of kind, generous jade
Melts my cold, stormy doubts with pleasant gestures
Of melodic elegance which gasps delight through me

Ensuring me that I will always know such wonderous riches
Amid this colorful world that God has created and given

Rich shades of robin egg blue and blushing rose murmur
Haunting my attention with joy that blends into the
Flamboyant imagination which gives life to the creation
And gentles the truth that God must bring us all a good
Gift, a treasured star, with this vista we call mother nature

The Light

The light shines in your eyes
Smiling and laughing
Teasing me with a vibrant beam
Caressing my thoughts
With music from the heart

The light whispers against bare
Skin, warming, energizing, invigorating
Reminding me that I can begin again
To hope and to pray, to believe
And to say . . . Love is alive inside

The light breathes gently through me
Embracing even the pain within
Coloring my soul in reflections of hope
Brightening my life with joy so alive
It penetrates my spirit with clarity

The light enlightens my deepest dreams
With hues of lavender sunsets and dawns
Flickering to the heavens in calm thought
Of all that has touched my heart and soul
With faith, hope and love that are forever

The Light is always alive, sending joy through my life

City of Lights

As the morning dawns and sunlight
Fades the darkness of night
Stars flicker out and moon turns to dust
And I recall the place of my heart
Here, I reside in Joyville, where I smile
Laugh and dance through the wonders

As noon rests against my bare skin
Caressing my heart with kindness
Whispering soothing thoughts
Into my soul and reminding me
That wherever I go there will always
Be this place for me, Heart City

As the night colors the entire world
In hues of soft grey and sapphire
Where flecks of stardust capture my
Spirit in a whirlwind of emotions
My heart races and praises with prayers
For the warmth of this city called Soulful

There are places I go when I do not know
Where the best place is . . . places like
Inspirational, Enlightenment and Yes, even
Despairsville . . . places I wander through
When my mind needs feeding and my thoughts
Need bleeding, like a feeling so vast and sure
It reaches past my calm and pierces my core

In these places, I know of the need
Need that is great and rides waves of hope
Lights flicker and create hues of flourishing
Caresses that mingle with mystery and music

Breaking out of the pain and sorrow and sending
Grace, mercy, peace and promise . . . love so reliable
It breathes inspirational poetry through my soul

And I reach past the echo of discouragement
Discovering the hand of healing, hope, happiness
That makes a way, even when the way seems impassable
A way through the city of Regret, Dark town and Sadville
Into the heart of praise, promise and psalms that pray
For a way through the weeds of wickedness and sin
Into the Garden of grace with Salvation that will win

Leave those dark cities behind and walk a mile to find
Joysville, Heart Town, Faith City and Love that Lasts
Discover the path to Light, love and laughter and you
Will find that this life can become something good
A part of your soul looks for this place where God
Gives the assurance that He is always with you, Guiding
You through and coloring your world in hues of pure love

Find your way – praise and pray – and you just may
Reach your destination and the home that awaits!

Hungry Prayer

There are prayers that we've been praying
Hoping hunger will somehow vanish away
Little hands held up to heaven obeying

Laughing and smiling, children are playing
In spite of hardship that leads them astray
There are prayers that we've been praying

Kind hearts whisper into small ears, saying
Just believe and God will answer you someday
Little hands held up to heaven obeying

Silent lights glimmer through nights, swaying
Listen to that still, small voice and obey
There are prayers that we've been praying

Gentleness and meekness call out, portraying
Warm, rich compassion like that on the Lord's day
Little hands held up to heaven obeying

Humanity lifts spirits who we should be repaying
Children who need love that we can't betray
There are prayers that we've been praying
Little hands held up to heaven obeying

He Died For Me

A true prayer is an inventory of needs, a catalog of necessities, an
exposure of secret wounds, a revelation of hidden poverty

C.H. SPURGEON

He died for me
Like the friend I could count on
To be there, fulfilling my needs,
When I was without a hope
And my thoughts were completely lost

He died for me
Like the One I could trust with my life
Knowing that love would put away all strife
Assuring my heart that I was precious
To the One who I call my Master

He died for me
Like grace, the living sacrifice
Answering my prayers, without even a doubt
That He would answer me
With a promise of restoration

He died for me
Like my last hope, my knowing
That life would not end
Because He came to be the ransom
For all my worst sin

He died for me
Like the answer to every prayer
For acceptance, joy and faith
That was fully aware I could be given
A life that was filled with compassion

He died for me
Like the wisdom from my heart
Piercing my pain with hope and comfort
A silent knowing that God would come
Back to me on that third day

He died for me
With only love to give to man
The truth that would assure them
God had a plan
And He would surely come back again

He died for me
And I know without a doubt
I am blessed as He rises in the clouds
Going back to heaven to give us the chance
To experience Jesus within us

With time, we will finally understand
The benefits of the Holy Spirit's flow
Within a soul who can always know
God is alive, living inside
Where He answers our prayers
With the assurance
That we have a friend within

We are blessed beyond
Our wildest dreams
With a love that is Jesus
Living in me, filling me to overflowing
With love that just keeps growing!

Love Alive

The laughter behind warm eyes
Twinkling with joy and delight
Imagining happiness only in dreams
Where this love lives unconditionally

Whispers of light inside a heart
Thriving with kindness, giving
Inspiration and assurance
That this love is completely fulfilling

Breathing gently against a heart
Hues of charity brought to life
By honest benevolence
Feelings grown through acceptance

Musical glories excite the heart
With melodies of pleasure
Sincerity and tenderness
Given through a gentle gift of faith

Miracles caress the spirit with love
Brought about by God's gift to us
His natural reward of prayer and praise
Honoring the love from which we are made

You bring my heart all the love I thought
Was gone from my life
Without a chance of coming back
Yet, you have given me a love that is so alive

It sings, dances and thrills
With a strength that encourages me to believe
There are always ways to reach beyond
The pain and sorrow we've been through

Discover the soothing love
That comforts, consoles and creates
A place of exhilaration and grace
From a God who completes our plans

For love that will always be
Never ending – eternally
Alive and thriving
On the inside

Fear

Fear whispers worry into your ear
Anxiety into your hopes and dreams
Fear promises to protect your heart
While it takes away your joy and faith

Fear keeps you awake at night
Yearning for the kindness of serenity
Within the heart who knows only dread
And the spirit who is living in panic

Fear lies to you with words of alarm
Spreads nightmares through your hopes
Breathes distress into your thoughts
And fills your life with apprehension

God whispers assurance into your ear
Words of joy through your senses
A promise of hope into your dreams
Confidence into your feelings of insecurity

God secures your soul with His love
Breaks apart trepidation with grace
Conceals your faith in a breath of praise
And awakens your joy with His Word

Listen to the whisper from above
Soothing and assuring your love
Reminding you to listen to God
Who knows all your fears and comforts you
Instead of allowing you to live in dread

Fear is a liar
Who will color your life
In darkness and distress
Follow God's light
And the voice of love's insight

Isaiah 41:10
King James Version
Fear thou not; for I am with thee: be not dismayed; for I am thy God: I will
strengthen thee; yea, I will help thee; yea, I will uphold thee with the right hand
of my righteousness.

Happy Easter

Light colors my heart
In a thriving breath of music
Touching my depths with compassion
That reminds me, surely, I know
The love that He bestowed
On my heart and soul

Laughter gentles my eyes
As they twinkle in amusement
Glorifying the grace that decides
My heavenly home, my paradise
The moment I will awake alive
With my guide, Jesus Christ

Love braves the cold
Sweetens my thoughts with kindness
That comes from knowing the one
Who lives inside my heart
Sending love through my thoughts
And awakening my hope

Living with the knowing
That He is alive, living inside
Brightening the future and breathing
Joy into the afterlife
Gives me assurance that I have faith
Which will touch me with grace

He is my answer to every question
The conclusion to my every prayer
The need that keeps me aware of
Inspiration, insight and intense appreciation
Of the One who died for me
And gave me the chance to be saved

Salvation came with a price
I could not pay
And it was paid by a God
I could not repay
He saves to the uttermost

Without any doubt
I know this Easter gives me the chance
To say "thank you"
For going to the cross – and especially
For rising again on the third day!

Happy Easter!

In A Glimpse

A glimpse of hope shined down
From the stardust promises
Of a Savior and a best friend
One who gave me deliverance
From the despair that filled me
With fear, doubt and dread
Darkness that shadowed my joy
Silhouettes of trepidation
Tormenting hope's blessings

A glimpse of light whispered
Across my heart and soul
Breathing colors in hues of summer
Sunshine yellow, bold scarlet
Flowing sapphire moon rising
Wrestling with the gloomy sadness
Blackening my heart with sorrow
Storming through my thoughts
With anxiety in flavors of failure

A glimpse of faith shimmered
Through the clouds of defeat
Welcoming gentle raindrops
All around the cloudless peaks
Where lavender mists with gray
Tails caught me up in the beauty
Of a rainy day, pouring out blessings
On me – through my Jesus' Love
Love that is unconditional, faithful

A glimpse of laughter healed me
From the loss and grief of mourning
When my heart ached with a yawning
Dread, a feeling so painful my prayers

Were fed by the comfort of knowing
Jesus is always with me, abiding
There inside my spirit – whispering
Miracles, compassion, dreams
Beauties beyond comparison, alive

A glimpse of love filled me up
With promises that I would know
Joy beyond compare, feelings
So rare and pure they traced
Kisses across the edges of rainbow
Dawns and embraced my soul
With expressions of serenity
And bold, brilliant thoughts
Of prayers and praise – eternally
Grateful for His mercy and grace

In a glimpse . . . Jesus knew
My heart, my soul, my truth
And He loved me through and through
With a love that is everlasting
With Him, I know the answers
Are found in His Word, where I meet
Him in so many verses of truth
Guiding me, assuring me, caressing me
With faith that knows He lives
Forgives and leads the way
To a heavenly home – where I'll
Spend eternity worshiping Him

In a glimpse . . .

Sin

Sin is a disease that destroys from
The darkness where it lingers
Always taunting us in the shadows
Of bitterness and dread, sinister
And haunting, calling out to the soul
For just a little more of its hope
Until all hope has been lost
And even faith and love are gone

Sin is ugly and angry and hateful
It prides itself on taking away
All the light that caresses a life
And stealing even the memories
Of laughter and joy, fulfillment
Found in colors of love breathing
Through a heart, whispering gently
Truth, inspiration and contentment

Sin is black and murky, obscuring itself
In the silhouettes of revulsion, disgust
That clings to the underbelly of evil
Thrusting its tentacles into corruption
Pleading with wickedness to continue
Producing sorrow and pain and regret
Remorse that remembers only the hues
Of somber gray that left a heart in fear

Sin is furious when it's discovered
And called upon to make itself known
To become a sin that is manifested
And adorned with the sacred blood
From the One who died to cleanse
Free the slave from the sinning

And release the captive with forgiveness
Absolution, pardon, clemency
Bought and paid for by the Son
Who died on calvary and rose up again
On the third day . . . to finally say

Our sin is under the blood
Forgiven, we can seek God's approval
Shun the darkness and begin again
To live in the light, where we can be seen
As a child of God, beloved and covered
By grace that has given us all the chance
To live for Jesus and enter heaven's sanctuary
Eternally blessed – a child of the best
God's grace is sufficient to save our souls
Allowing His love to make us whole

Ephesians 2:8–9
King James Version
[8] For by grace are ye saved through faith; and that not of yourselves: it is the gift
of God:
[9] Not of works, lest any man should boast.

Being Different

Not fitting in, I believe, is more blessing than curse – and not being like the rest of the pack is more fortunate than a smile or kiss. Are you one of the few who knows that being different isn't necessarily something to be ashamed of?

QUOTE BY POET

All the lonely people, the ones who live in fear
Of the loneliness that's taking them
Through anxiety and doubt, worries that haunt
And feelings that taunt the spirit
Are the ones who need to know for certain
They're loved beyond words or expression

All the mourning hearts, the ones who are in pain
Filled with sorrow that rests on their soul
Grief that teases and torments with dark thoughts
Leading their minds into anguish that aches
With weeping that whispers across naked wounds
In need of a light to brighten their gloom

All the ones who are different and wonder
Through this world with a dread for
The distinction that makes them seem a little
More wise or simple or any other alteration
These are the people in need of a kindness
From someone who can give without expectation

It is better to give than to receive – always
Give your smile to one in need of gentleness
Your embrace to one in need of a caress
Your encouragement to one in need of direction

Your light to one who is living in black dismay
Your love to one who is held up by their faith

Listening to Mom

Her lavender light shone bright
Surrounded my thoughts
With inspiration
Hope

Her gentleness whispered soft
Against my tender heart
With musical notes
Songs

Her kindness breathed life
All across my prayers
Soothing, caressing
Dreams

Her blushing rose rays of bliss
Sighed sensitivity within
With compassion that
Lives

Her brilliant wisdom, flourishing
Murmured hope and faith
Through my spirit's
Soaring

Her reflections of benevolence
Poured humility and humble
Love through my soul
Healing

Her truth came alive in praises
Of summer sun and starlight
Singing into the night
Vibrant

Her sparkle shone like diamonds
Shimmering through the noon
In sunlight echoes
Laughing

Her name was mom
I was her child
She was my
World!

Without her
I wouldn't be who I am today
I always am reminded to pray and praise
When I think of her loving ways

For you, my dear mom . . . I will always pray!

I'm His

I cherish the feelings I've known
The joys, hopes and dreams that have grown
From the depths of my heart and soul
Gentling my thoughts with emotions all my own
Love that leaves my affections completely whole

I cherish the family who have blessed my life
Encouraging and reassuring me through all my strife
Impressing my ambitions with sweetest serenity
Cutting through my worries with comfort like a sharp knife
Leaving me with an elated and thriving amenity

I cherish the inspirations that come from above
Dancing on the edges of my energy with richest love
Coloring me in hues of eager pleasure so sure
That I can't stop the sensations of laughter I'm in awe of
Despite all the trouble and sorrow this heart can endure

I cherish the wisdom which assures the mind
Everything that has been only a dream is a kind
Of happiness brought to life by the one who believes
God is there, lifting up with grace which is inclined
To bring a peace that only the soul perceives

I cherish God's beauty – His kindness and care
Giving that is so persuasive it is the answer to a prayer
Leaving even the silence filled with gentle belief
Bringing out the passion inside that will prepare
The breath of a promise within which brings such relief

I cherish God's tender gift of pure love
There is no greater gift that fits like a glove
On the one who knows what intimacy with the creator

Brings to the heart and soul who write of
Heavenly repose where the author is much greater

I cherish the sagacity of a reality
Where I know what it is to always agree
With the hopes that come from sweet praise
For the One who is always giving His joy to me
The one who knows that His love can always amaze

Above all that is and all that will be
I cherish God and will always bend my knee
To the One who I love beyond anything that is
To the One who breathed life into me
And gave me the wonder of surely being His

Compassion

Compassion smiles down
Like stars winking through the cosmos
Lifting spirits and warming hearts
Coloring the soul in a tune of light indigo
Hope whispering across my thoughts
Laughing love through my soul

Compassion lights my heart
Warm and wise, welcoming all thoughts
As they sift through the moments
Gentling my naked emotions
Healing me with a kiss, soft breath
Lingering on my fair skin

Compassion holds my dreams
In the curve of their teasing vibrancy
Echoing a prayer of gentle praise
Soothing my longing for serenity that frees
On the sunshine beams of music
With wings, free as the tendency to believe

Compassion caresses my memory
With moonlight hopes that thrill
Awakening my inner senses, breaking through
Wishes, worries, waste from wild
Faith – faith so alive it heals the hurts
Of a past which reminds you of remorse

Compassion burns like fire
Through the soul who knows
Passion and desire from the depths
Of a joy that brings about true yearning
For kindness that absorbs
Sorrow, angst, discouragement

Compassion thrills the sweet spirit
Of one who believes in the brilliance
Of a sunlight moment expressing itself
With gentleness and carefree
Sentiments that erase all the worst
Shading the thoughts with tenderness

Compassion breaks the promise
Of the one who vows to leave behind
The grief that troubles the mind
And brings mourning to the very soul
With the assurance that there is relief
In the elation that comes alive in tomorrow

Compassion is the breath of love
That breathes hope, faith and inspiration
Through the soul who knows
God is alive and wise and sure
More brilliant than ever before
And He knows . . . our deepest yearnings
As He pours out blessings across our souls

Malachi 3:10 KJV — Bring ye all the tithes into the storehouse, that there may be meat in mine house, and prove me now herewith, saith the LORD of hosts, if I will not open you the windows of heaven, and pour you out a blessing, that there shall not be room enough to receive it.

Love Changes Me

Love changes me from doubtful to hopeful
From down and out – to up in the clouds
From worried and anxious to happy and content
From lost in the sorrow
To inspired by the moments of grace

Love changes me from grief-stricken
To pleased and jubilant
From dark and dreary to light and cheery
From lost in the pain to grateful for the gain
From the shadows of disgust
To the enthusiasm of wanderlust

Love changes me from angry and bound by pride
To humble and willing to provide
For others more than myself, giving with a open spirit
Willing to accept whatever may come
With a open heart, in a spirit of sweet love

Love changes me from tense and agitated
To relaxed amid the glorious goodness
Of a life filled with fulfillment and beauty
Breathtaking rapture that satisfies the soul
Leaves the heart full of hope
And keeps the soul growing surer
Of a love that is God's promise of eternity

Love changes me from thankless and unpleasant
To grateful for the faith that gives me
Second chances, joy within and complete assurance
That I have His spirit to confide in
Speak to in prayer that will sustain and satisfy
Sincerely bless me with gratitude

Love changes me from one who is lost
To someone who knows the glory of hearts
Broken by conviction and accepted by His gift
Of freedom and salvation, the grace
That keeps me filled with a spirit who has been
Born again, lifted, accepted
By the God who created me and gave to me
His one and only Son, Jesus – my soul's promise
For pure unconditional love

Through faith, my heart is glorifying
In the love that changed me
And gave me . . . the chance to enter heaven's gate

Little Hands

Little hands lifted to the Lord
Praying and praising
Letting God know He's adored

Little hands raised to God
Hoping for a answer
To prayers that applaud

Little hands lifted up to the Lord
Sharing heart and soul
With the One who has restored

Little hands raised in faith
Reaching toward the heavens
Listening to what God saith

Little hands lifted to the Lord
Yearning for answers
To prayers filled with love of one accord

Little hands raised in trust
Knowing God will listen
To a prayer that is truly just

Little hands lifted to the Lord
Sure that God will answer
Solve the questions others have ignored

Little hands raised in praise
Thanking the God who created us
For giving us everything which does amaze

Sweet Children

Sweet children
Who reach out to a delicate dandelion
Blowing it's seed into the air
Whispering faith that this will bring
A answered wish or fulfilled prayer

Sweet children
Who smile at kittens and laugh
Listen to the chirp of birdsong like it is a caress
Giggle along with croaking frogs
And color the skies in lavender truth

Sweet children
Who listen to their hearts and sing
A brilliant tune with melody so kind and pretty
Lines that seem to bring peace in old age
And dreams to hope and faith

Sweet children
Who learn to believe in their visions
Of rainbows that linger on the imagination
Writing poetry on stardust and leaves
Of love expressed through belief

Sweet children
Who hug a puppy to their heart
Hoping they will never know the pangs of loss
Give thanks with a completely pure heart
And make life a better place to live

Sweet children
Who think spiders are their friends
Ache to know more about the giants and angels

Breathe harmony through laughing ideas
And make love seem like it's as simple as blinking

Sweet children
Who know they own my very heartbeat
As it trembles and pounds with sincere appreciation
For the breathless love that pours out of these
Who love without conditions and give complete thanksgiving

Sweet children
How I long to tell you
Your heart is like a caress
Your spirit is like a kiss
And your soul sings of Jesus

Calm

There is a peaceful place I visit
Where silence is a virtue
Life is just as gentle and tranquil
As the hues in a tangerine sunset

There is a quiet place I go to
When I'm in need of reflection
This place I mention is beautiful
And gives calm to my perspective

There is a still, soothing place I visit
Where light echoes brilliant love
Shining through the miracle of faith
And warming the heart with amazing grace

There is a clear, serene place I go to
When I'm hoping to discover kindness
Smooth against my naked thoughts
As tender as the whisper of the sea

There is a peaceful place I visit
Where joy sings to my soul
Breathing compassion through me
Like a comforting smile on the heart

He Gave Her A Book

Her Father was the Creator
Of the heavens and the earth
He gave her all of creation
Then, in time, He gave her
His word

The Bible was His precious
Book – of grace, faith and hope
Sprinkled in Love beyond measure
Love that could even be heard
In the scriptures He breathed
Light onto everything

His gift was more than blessing
It was wise beyond description
It was inspiration and enlightenment
A gift of purity and affection
Bringing life that was a living word
Written by inspired authors
Who knew she would soon need
This gift that surpassed her
Wildest dreams

Her Father gave her a book
And it was a book of wisdom and truth
Grace bound it up in love
And prayer brought it to birth
All her heart's hopes and desires
Her belief was like a warm fire
Sending tingles of love through her soul
And capturing her spirit in an embrace
From the psalms and praises
Flowing through the ink in His gift

The Word of God is alive
Breathing out passion for Him
The greatest giver there will ever be
The God of heaven, the Father
Of all creation

God, the Father
Gave her a book, the Bible
And it's contents – scriptures and verses
Are more potent and powerful
Than anything she could have imagined

With love, He blessed her greatly!

My Prayer for You

I pray you find peace
At the center of your soul
Where only God can know you
The way you should be known

I pray you find joy
To light your life and heart
Where there has been darkness
I pray joy ignites your brightness

I pray you find hope
To be and do your best
With grace to fill your mind
And bring glory to your thoughts

I pray you find faith
To guide you through the days
With assurance that you have grace
To flood your spirit with inspiration

I pray you find love
To warm your heart with compassion
Sending you into the heart's depths
With a promise of the everlasting

I pray you find this prayer
To remind you that you're cared for
That you deserve the best there is
Because you're truly a child of the King

My Thorn in the Flesh

I've made my share of mistakes
Failed many times – failure is loud
I've learned lessons from pain
And had to endure the darkness of rain
But through it all I've found that
Growth comes from lessons learned
Most often, from countless slip-ups

I have many faults I don't like
Little things – some not so small
Which reveal a part of me that
I would like to simply ignore is there
Leave it to God, who will answer a prayer
To remove this thorn in my side
Unless, like Paul . . . I'm meant to endure

I've slipped up now and then, friend
Without these bloopers, who knows?
I might never have learned what I was
Meant to learn, through mistakes
Errors as noisy as deafening screams
All those blunders that mark me as
So very human!! So very HUMBLE!

2 Corinthians 12:6–8 KJV
[6] For though I would desire to glory, I shall not be a fool; for I will say the truth:
but now I forbear, lest any man should think of me above that which he seeth me
to be, or that he heareth of me.
[7] And lest I should be exalted above measure through the abundance of the
revelations, there was given to me a thorn in the flesh, the messenger of Satan to
buffet me, lest I should be exalted above measure.
[8] For this thing I besought the Lord thrice, that it might depart from me.

Listen

Listen to your heart, your spirit
For the conscious revealing truth
The wisdom that comes from heeding
God's instruction, His correction
And His everlasting word, the Bible

Listen to the way He reveals to you
All the insight into a living devotion
Assurance that whatever you go through
You can find the answers in your soul
Where He guides, instructs and assures

Listen to His still, small voice – the light
That reflects His image, His Holy Spirit
Who welcomes you to praise and pray
In silence, in noise – wherever you may be
Yearning for God to take notice of your need

Listen to Him through the scriptures
Who reveal His heart and open the way
To receiving guidance and direction
Through sorrows, joys and everything
With promises for your benefit and help

Listen to the prudence of a heavenly Father
One who knows your deepest thoughts
Your secret dreams and all you believe
And find encouragement through His gift
Of reassurance and grace, inspiration and faith

Listen to your heart – listen to your intent
Do you hope to win or do you hope to give a gift?
Is your heart in the right place when you pray?

Do you hope to honor God and honor the faith?
Do you breathe worship through it all? Praise God

Listen to your soul, the part of you who knows
He is with you always – forever leading you on
Through sadness and sorrow, through joy and hope
Into the moments when you know you will discover
The answers to prayers and faith that is alive

Listen . . . listen.. to the still, small voice of God
Who looks past your anger and shame, your worst
To the center of your heart where He sees you
As you were meant to be seen . . . filled with a love
That dances and sings, love that was given by Him

Listen to your heart and believe in a love that is alive
Guiding your thoughts toward intimacy with the Lord
Who knows you need His love more than anything
And hopes you will come to Him through everything
Secure in the worship of One who is the light of your soul

Listen and know . . . God is still in control

1 Peter 3:16 KJV [16] Having a good conscience; that, whereas they speak evil of you, as of evildoers, they may be ashamed that falsely accuse your good conversation in Christ.

Pray

The best way to start you day
Is to Thank God and pray
For the chance to give a part of you
Your heart and soul, your love and hope

The best way to say you're thankful
Is to give back – always faithful
To the hearts who God gave you
To share your heart and time with

The best way to give your love away
Is to listen to the part of you that says
God's spirit is always living within
And giving you the chance to fully give

The best way to live your truth in life
Is to pray with a heart that gives and lights
Up the souls that come closest to understanding
Hope, faith and love are alive within you

The best way to prepare, reassure, amaze and yearn
Is to PRAY without ceasing for the grace to give
Back to heaven a piece of the wisdom it has given
Wisdom that says, God is great and we are His children!

The best way to PRAY is to always praise
With a open heart and a contrite spirit
With faith and hope – love that is living
With assurance that your soul is giving . . . .

Unconditional Love . . . love that is alive
And centered on the One who created us all
Made us to be souls who love and leave our mark
On the heart who knows that God is our only hope

He Knows Me

God loves me and I love God
God is love and love is God

God wrote me down
        On the empty page
Colored me vibrant
        All light and shadows

God pieced me together
        In hues of joy and pain
Whispered sunshine through me
        Erasing even the memory of rain

God embraced me with faith
        Assuring my soul of grace
Warming me in fires alive
        Passion, praise and prayer

God painted me in brightest hope
        Breathing kindness through my thoughts
Like wonders so satisfying
        They penetrate the depths of my feelings

God played music through my soul
        Singing a melody of starlight dreams
Across each kiss of the wind
        As it blows , breathless, on the lips

God planted me in fertile soil – love
        Nurturing me with tenderness
Soothing away every insecurity
        Dancing in rays of tangerine sunlight

His love lifts me up like exhilaration
       Shimmering through the night
Reflecting the inspiration
       That comes from a relationship
With the Father, Son and Holy Spirit

God is love and love is God
He is my Father and I am His child
I seek to know Him with every prayer
He knows me better than I'm even aware

The Light of God

Dancing through the trees
In blazing sunshine praise
Beams the light of a new dawn
Awakening hearts to remind
This is a second chance to become
The person you've always dreamed
You could be!

Blushing rays in tones of rose
Paint the soul in miracles who know
This is your opportunity to give
The world a part of your hope and
Faith, the part of you that is filled
With thanks for all the love you've
Known and all the love you've shown
Love that is alive in your soul!

Breathless thoughts whisper
Caressing your soul with feelings
Gentle and alive, like a teardrop
Chasing hopes on a path to the heart
Where there is goodness dreaming
Inspirations filling the mind
Clinging to the vine of enlightenment
Assuring the world that you own
The hope that lingers through you
To awaken other hearts to the knowing
That love is alive and pouring from
Hearts who know Him, the rising Son
The light of God!

In Nature

Lemon light whispering hope
Into the dawn
Joy into the breeze
Music into the gentle praise
Of One who created it all

Dewdrop dreams glimmering peace
Into the morning song
Coloring the heart in hues of faith
Inspirations so alive they abide
In grace, on the inside

Silent smiles from tulips and crocus
Striking the eyes
In haunting secrets that call
From the echoing paths
Along soft, sandy beaches

Lavender laughter delights
On the caress of a summer night
With stardust desire crying
Across the edges of compassion
Through the forest
Who captures truth praying
In tune to the mists falling

Breathing wishes through the thoughts
In passionate promises sought
By those who know love is alive
Thriving and abiding
On the inside of the one who knows
His spirit calls to us all
Through the beauty of a tangerine sun
And the miracle of a butterfly

Listen to the sigh of dandelion seeds
Being blown through meadows
Leaving starts of new life
Wherever they fall across black dirt
Nurtured by rain, bathed in the sun
Who knows that this is love
Although its just begun

Nature, in all it's glorious yearnings
Melts my heart and leaves me with assurance
That God is a creator, a artist, a master
One who knows life is more than air and water

Life is a caress from His spirit
Wise and warm and welcoming
The soul to partake of healing

With God, there is only fulfillment
Of the heart and soul
The promise of His indwelling
Giving love a label
A poetic tag
A inspirational term
His muse
Is my light and laughter
My prayer to the One who made me
And continues to amaze me

A Tree

I whisper to you on the morning breeze
Whistling, laughing and praising
Sharing my grace through the zephyr twists
A lasting murmur of light and love

I giggle with you in the afternoon light
Through lemony sun and fair clouds
Drifting with a trace of blushing roses
Lingering on my soft undertones

I pray to the heavens on wings of song
Coloring the moments in a longing of hope
For beauty that resides in the faith of a child
Leaving passion and promise on the silence

I brighten the days in inspiration that craves
Assurance on the tossing of my branches
As they wrestle with the moon and stars
Awakening love in the forest where I'm truly at home

I enliven the hearts of those who stroll on lawns
Where I'm at a part of the gentle panorama
Beckoning to the soul to know my sense of hope
When all my leaves are gone and I seem so weary

I bring life to the broken heart and soothe the distraught
With my dreamy hues of amber, gold and scarlet
During the autumn when my wardrobe is at its best
And I'm feeling free to let go and rest for a season

I'm Thankful

I'm thankful for the light of dawn
The beauty of a bird in song
The joy in a whispered psalm
The kindness beneath a warm smile

I'm thankful for the moon and stars
The breath of laughter clinging to love
The silence in the murmuring brook
The lavender that lights the skies with hope

I'm thankful for the dancing thoughts
The music beneath a lovely prayer
The heartbeat of joy within a giggle
The warmth that melts the hardest heart

I'm thankful for the hues of sweet grace
The exhilaration left beneath praise
The serenity within a gentle sigh of compassion
The crimson flow of God's gift to our souls

I'm thankful for every waking moment
The sand and sun – the mountain and tree
The softness beneath a tangerine sun
The echo of merriment coloring the fall

I'm thankful for the blessings I've known
The sense of calm that overwhelms my soul
The harmony of one who knows God's love
The faith that comes from knowing His Son

I'm thankful for every touch from His hand
The charity that sparks hope and wisdom
The benefits that are His for the giving
The insight of a soul who is filled with His spirit

Belief

Silence sings
     To the hungry soul
Baptizing night
     In whispers of moonlight

Painting the morning
     In a lemony sunshine
Breathing tenderness
     On butterfly wings

Gentling the storm
     With rain's sudden visit
Warming the winter
     By devoted fresh snowfall

Gathering the songs
     Of falling leaves who call
Laughing through minds
     Who hold onto their hope

Publishing poetic writes
     On pages awaiting insight
Lighting the heavens
     With a sense of praise

Overflowing sunset
     In brilliant rays of tangerine
Loving the addition
     Of grace and forgiveness

Leaving only healing
     On the hearts who are willing
To listen to God's spirit
     Who will reveal His indwelling

Love like this is real
 Filled with hope and giving
Second chances, new beginnings
 Grace that is fulfilling
Assurance that salvation is given
 To those who are willing
To follow God through time
 Into eternity to find
Hope, faith and love
 Are gifts from up above
And He has given us a peace
 That can quiet the deepest grief
Love like this
 Is the miracle of belief!

Life is But A Vapor

The moment we are born, take in our first air
We shorten our lives by a breath

In that first moment, that first breath . . .
We begin dying

If we live as we should, we live as if each moment
Every breath . . . is our last one
Our last hope, our last prayer
Our last thought, our last smile
Our last embrace, our last kiss
Our last feeling, Our last taste
Of a life that is our only chance

To give back a part of our heart
To a world that only knows us as
The one who danced with life, with love
As joyfully as the morning dove
Sent by the God who is above
Reminding us always that our life is but a vapor

What matters is the truth — That comes from the knowledge
That life only begins — When we're born again
And begin living life for Him

In God We Trust

On our dollars
We see the words
"In God We Trust"
Spelled out for us there
Across green currency
Is the hope that brings us
Insight into what our forefathers
Longed to see in our country

Since the tragedy of civil war
We've been known as
The United States
United being the word
That penetrates through our thoughts
To remind us that we aren't
Just Republicans or Democrats
We aren't a party
We are the UNITED states
If we live as we should . . .
Reminding ourselves that it is . . .

"In God we Trust"
And the
United States
We may discover that we have
The opportunity to share
Our thoughts, our hearts, our feelings
Without riots or demonstrations
But with kindness and consideration

Together, we might discover
We can get along with one another
Through faith in the God of love
And prayers sent up from us

To bring us back to the joined hope
That comes from sharing this land
And living in reverence and devotion
To the One who created every man!

God bless the USA

Breathing Silent Hope Through the Pain

Breathing silent hope through pain and its fears
Reaching past the sorrow to face the night
Learning to let go of hurt that haunts years
Lifting up one who's down so they can fight

Life's struggles sometimes overwhelm the plight
Show the world that hopes can be dashed by tears
Remind hearts that worries will dim the light
Breathing silent hope through pain and its fears

Loss soon will question the storm as it clears
Welcoming sunny skies that are so bright
Erasing the gray cloud who soon appears
Reaching past the sorrow to face the night

Dismal grief traps the soul who is in flight
Bringing despair as the dream disappears
Leaving sorrows that seem so filled with spite
Learning to let go of hurt that haunts years

Laughter becomes silent among these peers
Relief from troubles is full of insight
Yet no one can seem to ease hurt with cheers
Lifting up one who's down so they can fight

Yearnings for comfort come out as I write
The pain rains down like they are real pairs
To shadow spirits with dread full of fright
When will I find the grace of God who cares
                          Breathing silent hope through pain . . . .

A Humble Heart

I will discover hope — despite chaos
I will find the joy — despite the pain
I will find faith — despite the silence
I will find mercy — despite the rain
I will find the love — In a humble heart

A heart who is flooded
With kindness and warmth
A heart who knows goodness
Flows from the veins of one
Who gives without limits
Who listens to the soul
And finds their vision
Within the dance of feeling
That lights the heart with
Meaning, dreaming, fulfillment
Hope for comforting
Inspiration for adoring
Music for enlightenment

Love that fills and overflows
Spilling out through the universe
With ideas, insights, imaginings
Gasps of mesmerizing solace
Given to those who know well
The feeling of affection and worship
For the One who gave us all our
Purpose, our thoughts, feelings
Everything that reminds our heart
To feel, to give, to shine a light
From the very breath of life . . .
Illuminating the brilliance of a fire
Captured by God's gentle tug
On heartstrings who listen to

God's tender impressions of
Love that is forever alive, nourishing
Guiding and creating second chances
For our hearts to grow worthy of this
Feeling, this love that is alive, giving
Assurance, hope, inspiration that colors
Our entire world with breathtaking
Laughter, exhilaration, imagination
Joy that overflows the heart's veins
Bursting with rapture that will last!

Casting My Cares

You see the ugly scars
I see the beauty inside
You see the struggles and worries
I see the strength that makes it worth it
You see the pain and sorrow
I see second chances in the morning

Listen . . . to the touch of a pen
Who understands your need
To give back a piece of you
A part of your heart and soul
A chunk of your hope and faith
A sample of mercy and grace
Portions of your spirit's praise

Inspiration sings praises into
The kindness of a psalm
Portraying the evidence
Of hope that lingers on and on
Lifting up the dismal heart
With light, laughter and love
Whispered in the prayers
Of one who breathes in
The music of a sincere belief

If I were a star . . .
I'd look down to those soft wishes
Made on my twinkling shimmer
Enlightening the heart with a quiver
Of intimate hues that shadow the sparkle
With halos of pure, untainted love

You are the kindness beneath my concern
The victory that comes when I have won
The inspiration that brings my vision to life
The consideration that brightens even sunlight

Dear GOD

Know my heart, my mind, my soul
For You, my life is an open door
Lead me through the storms and strife
Remind me of your sacrifice

Know my hope, my faith, my prayer
Always make me fully aware
Of your grace, your light, your love
Every kindness from up above

Know my deepest insights and visions
The dreams that bring me joy and pleasure
Feelings and reflections that guide me on
Toward true peace and enlightenment

Know my needs, the things for which I plead
Direct my steps on the straight and narrow path
Show me how to pray with conviction
Light the way to salvation and contrition

Know my dance with joy and fulfillment
Send your light to shine upon my spirit
Grace my thoughts with tender affection
Draw me into the breath of your kiss

Know my strengths and my weakness
Share your power and wisdom to complete me
Fill me up with a love that lives eternally
And make me know the faith that fills my hunger

Know me, God, — Know my best and worst
Direct my feet on the path of joy and hope
Show me love that is wiser than the silent song
Whisper through my heart, inspiring me to go on

Toward the miracle of new birth and the Son
Who makes my life one I can be content with

Know me, God – Know me . . . all of me
Listen to my prayer for light that flows through me
Into the hearts that I meet on my way
To share your everlasting love and grace

I praise You, God . . . And Thank you for your mercy
You gave my heart a second chance
My soul the opportunity to share in faith
You know me better than I know myself!
Thank you, God – for Your marvelous kindness!

Forgiven

Learn to forgive even the one who didn't say they were sorry — forgive
from the heart, the soul, the spirit, with a forgiveness that is honest and fills
you with assurance that you are giving true love with forgiveness! – Quote
by poet

Forgiveness happens when a heart breathes
Light into another's darkness
Laughter into another's sorrow
Love into another's animosity

Forgiveness happens when you struggle
To feel more than faintly aware
Of the kindness that is in your prayers
For the one who made you feel so sad

Forgiveness happens when you write poetry
Through the tears someone caused
And find a way to thank them with your vision
Verses alive and shimmering with inspiration

Forgiveness happens when you long to touch
The naked thoughts of one who hurt you
Leave them flowing with a sense of delight
To remind them that you are always their ally

Forgiveness happens when you love unconditionally
With a love that hopes and believes and dreams
Love that is wise and teaches true faith
In the One who is the model of true mercy

Forgiveness happens when you reach out with faith
That the One inside your heart and soul
Is stronger and wiser than you could even know
And He will guide you to forgive without exception

Forgiveness happens when you know your heart is broken
But you also know your love is worth it – you're hurting
But you're bound to give complete absolution to the one
Who hurt you because you know, without a doubt . . .

That love this strong was inspired by the One
Who forgives more than words can say, more than grace
Can possibly think and more than faith can trace . . .
Love like this forgives because it knows forgiveness
True forgiveness . . . is found in the shadow of a cross
A cross at calvary where Jesus paid it all for us

God is in Control

When life brings you to a place
Where pain and sorrow you must face
Listen to the wind and rain, leave a smile
From the stardust thoughts that whisper
Grace across your soul, lighting the way
So you can know how to let go of your tears

When life leaves you feeling sad
And nothing on earth feels quite this bad
Breathe a promise into the sand and sea
Lavender hues of promise and prayer
Soothing away all the worries you've had
And reminding you to always listen and care

When life brings you flavors of anger and hate
Laugh at these moments that are your sure fate
Lighten your heart with moonlight dreams
And caress the kindness written on the night
Painting the stars in a dazzling mystery
Filled with silent inspirations that sigh with wonder

When life publishes poetry through the air
Caressing your naked fancy with a sense so rare
Sunshine and butterflies – birds that haunt
With their songs so alive, colorful and bright
Leaving music that peppers thoughts with calm
Flavors so soothing they linger on and on

When life darkens your faith and dims your dreams
Awakening the apprehension with trouble that screams
Rousing the sense of yearning within an anxious soul
Delivering suspicion and fear, leaving hearts aware
That even in the greatest moments there are silhouettes
Shaded in dread, fretting and distress – unease and unrest

When life sounds like thunder beating against your hope
And you can't find a way through the struggles to cope
Know that God is with you, a flicker of courage in the dark
Preparing you for the day when you'll see this effort
As merely a battle that was meant to teach you how
To learn and grow, to know – you can always rely on God

The truth of His love is beyond explanation
His love is alive, like the joy I feel on the inside
When I sense His gentle kiss on my open heart
And long for the still, calm touch of His hand
When He traces a path through my crimson veins
Into my laughter, my life, my love – into my soul

Where God is in full control!

Vanishing Values

"All change is not growth, as all movement is not forward."
—ELLEN GLASGOW

The old ways of life are like an endangered species
Lost in the cycle of life that brings us more
More houses, more jobs, more value . . . or
Does that really mean less — if the truth were spoken

There was a time when we all shared our meals
Around a kitchen table where hope dwelled
There we prayed, learned and grew strong
From home cooked meals served with honest love

There was a time when we knew right from wrong
We didn't need any instructions other than God's word
To remind us that we were doing something sinful
Losing our morals or damaging our values for some indulgence

Is it valuable enough to call it worthy, meaningful and alive
Like the past we've left behind along with God's authority

Real Beauty

You see the ugly scars
I see the beauty inside
You see the struggles and worries
I see the strength that makes it worth it
You see the pain and sorrow
I see second chances in the morning

Where you only see the despair
I see the value of time spent
Reflecting on what is most important
The heart and soul – the dreams within
The joy that comes from knowing
God's grace is always there for us

You see the grief and mourning
That comes from death's calling
I see the love that brought life
To the soul who has gone on
The breath of joy given to those
Who know death isn't really the end

Where you see only the decay
Left behind by autumnal arrays
I see the fiery oak, maple and birch
All of those heavenly displays
That brought us such amazing sights
Whispers of laughter in the starry nights

You see the darkness in the evening
While I see only the deep silence
Revealing soft feelings so powerful
They remind me that I have been blessed
By the kind caress of answered prayers
The happy thoughts within God's breath

Where you see the pain that thrives
Breaking both hearts and minds
I see the lessons that have been learned
Taught by the anguish of a soul
Who knows that God will reassure
With renewed faith, hope and love

Salt of the Earth

Salt is the seasoning, the spice of life
The reason for giving out
Flavors to heal hurt
Herbs to relieve grief
Suggestions that fill minds
With hope, faith and love

Salt is the zest of giving
The tang that touches
Upon the heart's feelings
The additive that suggests
We all need God's healing
With the adoring light of living

Salt is the flavoring, the hint of
Hope that rises inside one
Who knows that love is there
Alive on the inside of the soul
Where the Holy Spirit lives
And guides us toward much more

Salt is the sense of truth
That beckons to our minds
Heavenly suggestions of joy
Inspiring the spirit to delight
In the wisdom of sending out
Laughter, smiles and insight

Salt is the aroma of tears and sunshine
The grasp of feeling inside one
Who knows that faith is alive
Providing a sense of assurance
Insight into the scriptural blessings
That thrive with pure inspiration

Salt is the touch of color pouring down
From the edge of the rainbow
From beginning to end, shades
Of pastel gentleness relieving souls
Of the sorrow, worry and fear
Sending love through that stunning arc

Salt is the essence of God's breath
Sighing with the whisper of a caress
Gentle appreciation sent down to us
Who know that He lives and sends us
Quiet joy, hope, faith, serenity and more
To fill us up with unconditional love

Matthew 5:13 King James Version
[13] Ye are the salt of the earth: but if the salt have lost his savour, wherewith shall
it be salted? it is thenceforth good for nothing, but to be cast out, and to be trod-
den under foot of men.

I'm Thankful

I'm thankful for His tender mercies and grace
The breath of faith that I always seem to embrace

I'm thankful for His compassionate whisper of love
The feelings that keep me filled with joy from above

I'm thankful for His wisdom, strength and kind word
His sympathetic nature assures me that I am heard

I'm thankful for His comfort when I'm living in fear
The miracle of His encouragement helps me all year

I'm thankful for His answers to all of my prayers
The inspirational truths that relieve all my cares

I'm thankful for His kindness which sings to my soul
Creating a purity within me that makes me feel whole

I'm thankful for His knowledge that sends me hope
Warming my plans with words to help me to cope

I'm thankful for His loving spirit which welcomes me
Promising me that I am loved beyond what I can see

I'm thankful for His glorious rays of the sun and Son
Who guides me toward home when my race is won

I'm thankful for the chance to give back a small part
Of all the love I've been given by One inside my heart

Prayer and Praise

I give Him my heart, my soul and my thoughts
    All of my worries, doubts and fears
I give Him all even though I'm tied up in knots
    Longing for a second chance to begin

I give Him my light, my laughter, my love
    All of my joy and all of my warmth
I give Him the kindness brought from above
    To give to others – assurance of hope

I give Him my questions, my yearnings and tears
    All of the reasons I can't find my way
I give Him my dreams, my fantasies and cares
    Speaking to Him of feelings I can't let go of

I give Him my nature, my thoughts and belief
    All the thoughts that seem to haunt me
I give Him my troubles, my sorrows and grief
    The dread that reveals my deepest phobia

I give Him my mornings, my noon and my night
    All of my feelings that inspire me to try
I give Him my moments filled with so much insight
    Welcoming me to give generously

I give Him my whispers of imagination and truth
    All the happiness that protects my spirit
I give Him my breath of harmony from my youth
    The dance of wonder that mends my aches

I give Him my reflections of all the mercy and grace
    All the supplications that have been answered
I give Him my life so that my sins He can erase
    Giving me a new enthusiasm for prayer and praise

Acoustic Visions

Acoustic visions that I had rejected
Brightening hearts with dreams perfected

Whispering faith through my soul
With lavender wishes that would console

Painting affection across my thoughts
Leaving my feelings tied up in knots

Caressing my smile so that it is amplified
Gracing eternal hopes that would abide

Guitar images glide through my mind
Enriching my life with joy and love combined

Music so wise it lifts the broken hearted
With a melody so alive it is uncharted

Notes ring and cling to the edges of my mind
Where the breaths of harmony are so very kind

Playing out the praises that drift to God's ear
Lighting up the heavens with love He can hear

Making a joyful noise that rings life to the harkening
Echoing through hearts, lighting where it's darkening

Gentle songs and hymns grace the longing heart
With joy, hope and love that God does impart

Through the caress of a voice ringing with wonders
Rain or sun, the embrace of the chorus thunders

Sounds of laughter kissing the choir with delight
Ringing through the sweet moments into the twilight

Without this caress from the voices so alive with joy
There would be no blessed tune for God to enjoy

Praising with the cry that drifts up to His throne
With voices that vibrate with the light they've shown

Whispers of Grace

Inspiration sings praises into
The kindness of a psalm
Portraying the evidence
Of hope that lingers on and on
Lifting up the dismal heart
With light, laughter and love
Whispered in the prayers
Of one who breathes in
The music of a sincere belief
Faith that caresses the soul
With hope that is alive and sure
Giving light to the heart
And laughter to the hurt
Caressing the spirit with a promise
Of serenity, sincerity, sensitivity
The assurance that love will shine
Bright into the darkest storm
Bringing alive the dance of hope
And warming the heart with
Adoration and calm, tenderness
That breathes joy into the one
Who listens to God's voice
Whispers of grace from the One
Who gave us all the blessing
Of His Son, Jesus the Messiah
The answer to our doubts and fears
The One who would bring us all
Compassion that lifts the broken
Heals the defeated and leaves peace
To the heart who needs freedom
His love is the answer to a prayer
Prayed by lips in need of more
Than a mere touch or word or deed

But, a trickle of the holy blood
Which covers every sin and shame
Relieves the sorrows and keeps alive
The whispers of God's grace!

Soul Songs

Growing a rose, blushing
Shy as the dawn
Awakening
Hope

Drinking the sea, sapphire
Warm like the summer
Glimmering
Grace

Dancing in the breeze, twirling
Whispering soft poetry
Caressing hearts
Faith

Breathing notes, melody
In hues of melancholy
Misty azure
Silence

Laughing lights, stars
Glimmering on black
Backdrops
Nocturnal

Dreaming elation, salvation
Miracles praising
In the air
Love

Creating music, composition
Details blended
Inspiration
Gentle

Breaking up prisons
Of inhibitions
Naked desire
Passion

Brilliant and vibrant, captivating
Sunshine gold, feathery
Feelings glide
Spirituality

Roses grow wise, welcoming
Capturing promises
On petals
Delicate

Sensations of joy, fulfilling
Hearts breaking
Connecting, soul
Songs

If I Were A Star

If I were a star, lighting up the night
Filling hearts with joy and hope
Inspiring souls to listen to the silence
That breathes a caress across the spirit
Whispering kindness to the listener

If I were a star . . .

I'd look down to those soft wishes
Made on my twinkling shimmer
Enlightening the heart with a quiver
Of intimate hues that shadow the sparkle
With halos of pure, untainted love

If I were a star . . .

Famous for the wishes that come true
After they've been given a sigh to
Encourage the believer to keep trusting
Imagining, creating, giving and praising
With a heart that knows unending faith

If I were a star . . .

I'd answer the heart who truly heard
My plea for them to give all they could
From the kindliness, where joy withstood
The test of time, trial and tribulation
Growing more alive and more faithful

If I were a star . . .

My fame would be told all over the world
Reminding the one who takes a moment
To murmur a prayer, a hope, a wish
For inspiration, serenity and grace
To be a way of life, a reason for praise

If I were a star . . .

I'd reach out to you wherever you are
And free your doubts from their gloom
Revealing the wonder found in truth
The pearls of great worth discovered
Inside the one who believes, never giving up

If I were a star, glittering and shining
Across the darkest sky . . . reflecting the vibrant
Dance of glistening, lively luminosities
I would scatter charms of elation wherever
My light happened to blaze with its flame of euphoria

If I were a star, as famous as the sun and moon
I'd reach out to your heart with the hope
That you would listen to the light of my reflection
And know that you are someone deserving
Of all my dazzling, glistening, flashing exhibits

If I were a star . . .

I would know the answers to all of your dreams
I'd reach out to you with happiness that fills
Comforting your heart, coloring your soul
In shades of laughter, lighting up your world
With my flawless smile of goodness and charm

If I were a star . . .

My fame would surely light up your thoughts
Brighten your hopes with assurance and warmth
Bring feathery wishes to their realization
Satisfying desires and reassuring all yearnings
That their wishes were heard and secured

If I were a star . . .

I would live for the gift of giving back to you
A small part of the joy that comes to me
When you lift up your lips toward the heavens
And breathe a longing from your breast
I live for the gift of your tender request

Prayers For You

I pray for you to be blessed
With sunshine that has confessed

To giving an embrace to your soul
With love that will make you whole

I pray for you to be given hope
With kindness to help you cope

Whispering a kiss of gentle light
That penetrates the darkest night

I pray for you to find inspiration
With joy that creates pure elation

Breathing kindness through your heart
In rays of faith that brings a new start

I pray for you to light up the world
In hues of gold and scarlet swirled

To bring sweetest silence from thoughts
So jubilant they tie one up in knots

I pray for you to know tender peace
Serenity that can only continue to increase

As it beckons to the music of the wind
Which is left with only its vision defined

I pray for you to realize every dream
Caressing your heart with its stream

Reassuring the prescient of honest belief
That will only bring the greatest relief

I pray for you to know that you are loved
From the heavenly hand which is gloved

With empathy, sympathy and concern
That will always help you to grow and learn

I pray for you to know what it is to give
As God shows you the best way to live

Comes from offering pieces of yourself
Instead of leaving the heart upon a shelf

I pray for you to reach out with desire
To stoke the flames of love a little higher

Nurturing the tenderness until it overflows
Leaving only light to brighten the shadows

God Lives

In the shadows, beneath the darkness
Hides a whisper of silent heartbreak
Reflecting mourning that rises within
Where there is little more than a breath
Of melancholy that persuades my spirit
To listen to the music echoing inside
As I dance to the colors of God's verses
Ending the pain, the sorrow and grief
The longing for a moment of reprieve

In the silhouette of a happy hope
Lingers a feeling of joy so tantalizing
It mirrors the grace found in the soul
Who knows that their worth is realized
In their relationship with God above
The One who gives the answer to all
The prayers they have spoken to Him
With the assurance that He will bring
Answers that color the heart in relief

In the hues of sapphire faith and grace
There lives a million moments of longing
For the chance to reach out to someone
With inspiration, encouragement, assurance
That the light of love lingers on in the one
Who listens to the scripture's blessings
And smiles with a hint of peace and fulfillment
Found inside the heart and soul of those
Who know God is always in control of it all

In the light, beneath the glowing insight
Shrouds a sense of reassurance that comes
From knowing that there is wisdom and strength
In the kindness that God gives His children

There is sincerity and warmth within the one
Who carries the Word to those who need to know
God is alive . . . He thrives and survives
Every loss, each problem, every difficulty
He lives to give His children the gift of true love

Praise God

He's writing my story
On the pages of this life
Creating each chapter
With hues of insight and light
Brilliant rays of joy, captured on
Words that come alive
When they've been given the gift
Of their introduction to Jesus Christ

He's writing my story
With a pen dipped in His blood
Dripping hope and faith
Sharing the ecstasy of grace
Welcoming the heart and soul
To a meal of peace and joy
Filling up the weakest child
With strength from His redemption

He's writing my story
With compassion between each line
Whispering inspiration and insight
Through the pieces of my thoughts
Leaving verses and rhymes
That create stanzas of vibrant strokes
Brushed across the intriguing dreams
Left smiling in eyes who know the Savior

He's writing my story
On sheets of silent sighs
Breathing laughter and pleasure
Into the hearts who touch upon
The knowing, the assurance
That He has opened the heart

To give love that can only come
From a personal relationship with God's Son

He's writing my story
Reaching down to edit the phrases
When my prayers beg Him
For more faith that I might have
More hope than I can expect
More love than I ever had

He's writing my story
And I'm seeking Him through prayer
For a intimacy with Him
That can only be felt by the heart
Who can feel His pen pressing down
Writing words that come alive by His mark

He's writing my story
And I am living proof
That every word He's written
Has left me more assured
That God is always good
God is always praiseworthy

Praise God!!!!

Grace

Despite my sin and failures
Which haunted and taunted my spirit
He loves me deeply
With a love that is living
Thriving and giving
From the heart of the Master
Love that brings with it
Hope, faith and serenity
Love like this is penetrating
Enlivening, inspiring, thrilling
Love like this is beyond imagining
It is the answer to many prayers
Pleas for the feelings
That bring assurance over doubt
Kindness over insolence
Warmth over the callous heart

Despite my faults and flaws
Everything that makes me wrong
He loves me with a love
That is so alive it sings a melody
Of joy, a promise of strength and wisdom
That comes from listening to that
Still, small voice . . . God's breath
Breathing out a gentle direction
For keeping faith at the center
Of all that I enter into

Despite my worst wickedness
The crimes I've been overcome with
There is grace that He lends me
Thru faith where He sends me
To the empty tomb, where Jesus left me
A miracle that would give me the chance

To look toward the heavens and know
I will go there one day, after a time
After I have moved from this body
To the spirit world where the Father
Will welcome me into His haven
With the Son who gave me the hope
That keeps me focused on the moment
When I meet Him in the sky
Welcoming with an embrace
Filled with sincerity and mercy

And I praise Him . . .

There is . . .
Light that shines across my soul
Letting me know that I have discovered
God's most joyful gift,
The rich and vibrant place called
Heaven, the home in the sky
Where you and I are invited
After we leave this world knowing
That His Son has died for our souls
And He is there, awaiting us
The ones who have been filled with
The spirit that gives off that light
Of redemption, salvation, elation
Love that is unconditional!

Ephesians 2:8 — For by grace are ye saved through faith; and that not of your-
selves: it is the gift of God

Rain Song

Splattering, splashing, sputtering
Droplets wet everything, everywhere
Spraying waters in wishes, reflections
Captured amid the depths of puddles
Mirroring the gentle flow of liquid
With hues of dampened, drenching
Sentiments, sensations, sweet soothing
Sounds of rain covering the surface
Of cool, black earth – running away
On seas of flowing energies, soul
Quenching streams of translucent
Vitality, power and strength, vibrancy
Coming alive in the hues of soaked
Impressions, ambiances, perceptions
Of glorious grace, praying in the swells
Of pools filled with light caresses
Fondling, kissing away all melancholy
With damp dreams of a future joy
Rising across the azure sky, echoing
In rays of a fresh, stirring sunshine
Lighting the way for morning praises
From the heart of one who knows
God lives in the rain as well as the sun
Leaving His signature in the arc
Of that vibrant, intriguing bow
After the clouds have moved on

Genesis 9:16 — And the bow shall be in the cloud; and I will look upon it, that I may remember the everlasting covenant between God and every living creature of all flesh that [is] upon the earth.

In The Silence

In the silence of the darkest night
Whispering serenity through my soul
There comes a hope so wonderful
It is alive, thriving, surviving all loss
With the assurance that there is love
Love that builds bridges to tomorrow
And heals pain with a salve of kindness
Creates compassion from joy and faith
Leaves only a breath of doubt behind
Where it can say it has been and gone
Leaving only reassurance to carry on

In the silence of the final note of a song
Dancing softly through the right and wrong
Glorifying the creator who knows our heart
And gives us the gift of His beloved Son
To guide us forward, through pain and sorrow
Into a world that is filled with worry and fear
Dread that what is will forever be there
Darkening the sunrise with distrust and disgrace
Filling up the moments with disappointment
Leaving only grief to color the world
In hues of steely gray that beckons the way
Toward doubt, confusion and disdain

In the silence of the freshly fallen snow
There comes a purity that innocence knows
Is the reflection of hope, faith and love
These three who capture the wonder of life
Leaving out all trouble, apprehension and strife
Filling up the moments with grace and mercy
Wiping away the tears that fall like dew on roses
Clinging to the cheeks of those who know
Only the jewels that caress the spirit with tender

Prayers, pleas for forgiveness, will discover
The answer to it all is found with faith in the One
Who knows our hearts and souls and loves
Unconditionally, completely, without reason
With a love that is always in season
Saving us from the horrors of life without hope
A life that knows Jesus is a life that can cope

Gaining My Wings

Fear gripped my soul
When I contemplated
Doing that new thing . . .
. . . and I asked God
"What if I fail?"
He answered softly,
"Dear child, what if . . .
You gain your wings?"

And I remembered why
He is the God I turn to
For insight and inspiration
Assurance and encouragement
Light, love and laughter

Everything that is good
Comes to me from Him
Who grants me grace and mercy
With a love that keeps me filled
With praise and worship
For Him who makes my life
Worth everything that comes

God sought me, bought me
And taught me . . .
In the end, He is my best friend

Light and Love

Breathing light
Across the darkest night
With whispers of joy
Filling the heart and soul
With a dance of kindness
In hues of lavender
With the miracle of love
Soothing dreams
Awakening feelings
Freeing ideas
To bring out the intimacy
That comes from sweetening
The moments with sugars
Of hope, faith and love
Singing visions from above

In the light there is insight
Stirring sensations of desire
Passion and fire that comes alive
On the heart who beats in a crimson
Flow of inspiration, ideas, belief
Through the veins of compassion
Gushes a prayer for eternity

In love – there is light
In light – there is love

Together, the two are one
Wispy, feathery caress
On the tune of blessings
From God's powerful presence

It Is In God's Hand

May every dawn bring the sun's light of love
May every thought bring hope for the heart
May every dream bring serenity and faith
May every strength give grace that relieves
May every doubt come with a probably can

I wish you all the joy that can be found in the sunrise
I wish you all the happiness that can be found in wisdom
I wish you all the harmony that can be found in music
I wish you all the inspiration that can be found in loving
I wish you all the kindness that can be found in a heart

You are the whisper of compassion that rises in my thoughts
The gentle humility that covers all doubts or worries
You are the breath of insight that melts away all hardness
The enlightenment that brings me through the darkness
You are the brush of hope that colors my entire world in love

As you walk through this life, know that I am behind you
With a prayer for your happiness, encouragement and delight
The feeling that this world has been blessed by you
The one who gives life a chance to express all it has
With assurance that the dance will always bring exhilaration

As you live, learn and grow . . . I hope that you will always find
The answers to your prayers are there inside your heart
Giving you all the intuition you might need to reach out
And discover your dreams are there within your grasp
All you need to make them come true is a touch from God's hand

Dancing Joy

Dancing through the moments, peppered with joy and kindness,
I find relief — I find love–
QUOTE BY THE POET

Like a lonely piece of history
Discovered on the edge of the forest
In a old oak tree, upon a gray branch
Knots painted in somber, ashen hues
Caressing the bird as it sings praises
Praying soothing melodies
Across the woods
On winds of
Joy . . .

My heart finds serenity
On the winds that caress and breath
Remembrance through the trees
Calming my soul with grace
Mercy that reigns free
Taking me to hope
For the moments
When I fly
Across
The
Sky . . .

With the light of love
Lost in the glimmering truth
Of a heart who is home
To my dreams, my faith
Brightening the way for the day
When I find inspiration alive
Dancing through desire
With a fire that flames
Heartfelt love
Lasting
Insight

When I reach through the moments
With my prayers, my longing
I find a sense of peace
That comes from
Knowing God
Is there
With me
Alive

He burns away the erosion
With a hand of affection
And I worship Him
With assurance
That He is
The answer
To my
Aching for
Love

Wildfire

He knows what the future holds
As He knows the here and now
He knows every small detail of
My heart, soul and spirit's doubts
He knows about my sorrows and pains
Has healing in His every mercy
Gives me the opportunity to share
The feelings of my heart's depths
The wonders that fill my dreams
The joy I feel when I think of Him

He knows about my fears and worries
Sees all the thoughts going through my head
Helps me to work up the needed courage
To face all my struggles with assurance
He knows how deeply I yearn for affection
And how I love to give love to others
Sees when I'm going in the wrong direction
Guides me through the unsuitable paths
Onto better avenues of joy and wonder

He knows about all my hopes and dreams
How I value the love I find in my family
He sees the pain that haunts me whenever
Some sadness reaches out to a loved one
Breathes sorrow through the black clouds
That surround the heart who knows that
Love can be destroyed by doubt and loathing
Feelings that cause hearts to quack and break
From all the pain that cuts through the essence
Of one who longs for the joy of compassion

He knows what will happen before it ever does
Reaches down with His care before we feel
The pangs of pain and doubt that will come
When sorrow beckons us from the ruins of the ache
Found within a soul who holds on to the sting
of a wound that continues to penetrate the soul
with throbbing soreness that resembles torture
He is the only One capable of taking away
That grief that comes from the deepest of pain
When there is anguish that will not let go

He knows about us – our depths, heart and soul
Everything we think – everything we are
He knows our spirit's wonders and wants
The hues of light that surround us with warmth
When we meet grace and find the way
Toward letting go of the sadness and reaching out
To the gladness – the gift of His presence
Piercing our soul with the knowledge that
We are loved more than we can ever know
With a love that is stronger than any hurt
A love that grows wiser with time and trial
Leaving our lives filled with sensations of thrills
Felt when God blesses a heart with a prayer
For giving from the heart the gift of His love
Love that is the answer to every worry or doubt
Love that sends hope to the hopeless
Love that brings light to the darkness
Love that lingers throughout the sad times
Love that shares life with mercy and grace
Love that is alive, dancing like wildfire

Abide These Three

And now abideth faith, hope, charity, these three;
but the greatest of these is charity.

1 CORINTHIANS 13:13

Faith is the answer to our heart's prayers
For a reason to breath inspiration through
The soul who longs for more than words
More than deeds – more than mere dreams
The soul who yearns for a strength and peace
That comes from listening to the Holy Spirit
Whispering faith into our hearts and souls

Hope is the answer to our fears of failure
The ones that cause us to worry and agonize
Over things we can't control, change or trade'
For better things like happiness, joy and inspiration
Hues of heavenly grace that exceeds our expectations
For a light that would shine through the night
Dancing in reflections of gentle hope that beckons

Love is the answer to our spiritual suspicions
The ones that erase our laughter and smiles
Find a way to paint darkness across our lives
Finally, love brings to life the assurance that it
Can warm the coldest heart with feelings of serenity
Enlighten the cloudy doubts and encourage souls
To believe in the One who lived and died for love

These three, . . . faith, hope and love – were sent to us
On a promise from above that we would be given
All we need to live our lives in unison with His voice
Recognizing the joy that comes from always listening

To the One who created us and makes life worthwhile
Giving us the sensitivity to enjoy His love with a smile
Of thanks and praise which rises from the humble heart

Silent Psalms

The LORD is my strength and my shield; my heart trusted in him,
and I am helped: therefore my heart greatly rejoiceth; and with my
song will I praise him.

PSALM 28:7

In the silence
Breath of hope
Whisper of faith
Mystery of grace
Dances through the soul
In hues of amber, crimson and gold
Wrapping the heart in warmth
From the light that rises across the sea
When there are thoughts filling the mind
With Jesus, God's precious Son

In the stillness
Sighing with dreams
Murmuring inspiration
Making way for belief
Swirls freely, with praise
In moments of humility, modesty
Chasing away the darkness
With reflections of starlight
Capturing the heart's promises
With rays of truth and consolation
Discovered in the knowledge that
Jesus is the light of the world

In the quiet
Panting psalms and poems
Praises of the One who
Lives to teach us the truth
Assure us of our own worth
Remind us that we can love
Beyond the pain and hurt
Past the grief, worry and fear
Through the most horrible nightmare
Into the heart of the moment
When we look joy in the eyes
And know – God is always in control
Of our lives!

She is a Warrior

Wait on the LORD: be of good courage, and he shall strengthen thine
heart: wait, I say, on the LORD.

PSALM 27:14

She was a warrior with a fearless spirit
She listened to the Lord – the still, small voice
She was a fighter with a valiant nature
She listened to the Lord – went the way of the Cross

There never was a time when she felt brave
And there were many moments when she felt defeated
Like her heart would break and her soul would fail her
But, like a light that shines through the darkness
His flame twinkled through the shadows of sorrow
Left her feeling like He had touched her with courage
Inspired her to live a little closer to Him, closer in
Where she was always so sure she had a real friend

She was a trooper with a heroic demeanor
She followed Him through the worries and troubles
She was brave with a heart that whispered keep giving
She followed His counsel and learned to about living

There never came a day when she felt like she could pay
The price for all that sin – but when she entered in
To the relationship with Jesus, the One who died for her
She was given a second chance to live a life meant for good
A life built on hope, faith and love and goodness from above
A life God inspired her to live, without worry or dread
With the gift of the Holy Spirit to breathe serenity within
Where Jesus gave her the assurance that He would always be
There for her, lighting the way, helping her to stay strong

She was a warrior with a fearless spirit
She listened to the Lord – the still, small voice
Who directed her to love unconditionally
With a love He spoke into her spirit

His Peace

O Lord our God, grant us grace to desire you with a whole heart, that
so desiring you, we may seek you and find you; and finding you, may
love you; and loving you, may hate those sins from which you have
redeemed us, for Jesus Christ's sake.

—ANSELM

Come to me in the silence of the night
As stars glitter across a shadowy sky
Breathe whispers of hope into my soul
With rhythms of heartbeats throbbing
Hues of laughter in colorful collections
Of gentle truth, erasing fear and worry
Praising the Creator of all this beauty
Surrounding us with brilliant spontaneity
Love that beams across the meadows
In lavender sighs, shining music into eyes
Who know the warmth found in a life
That has learned to thrive and survive
Even the worst loss of hope and faith
Leaning on the power of amazing grace
That flows through veins of compassion
Enlightening, enchanting, enticing joy
To pray for the dance that will attract
Feelings rich and penetrating, alive
With passion that lights a flame
Energizing the spirit with flickering
Smiles that radiate through life
Warming hearts and welcoming thoughts
Of bright enthusiasm and cheerfulness
Hope that fills the morning with sunshine
And the evening with dewdrop dreams

Like little touches of heaven sent down
To remind us all that God sends to us
Love that is fully alive and electrifying
Igniting a fire, rousing desire, inspiring
The heart and soul to awaken joy
Who will paint life with glitter and wonder
Awesome, exhilarating, exciting thoughts
Brought into a mind who is wise beyond words
Because it knows the meaning of life
Is more than ideas, thoughts or words
The true meaning of this life we spend on earth
Is in representing the One who died for us
That we might live life in the way
It was meant for us to live it!

Praise God for His gift of this Son
The One who left us with a hope to lean on
When dark days bring dread of what is
And worries of what is to be . . . . . . in eternity
Thank God for His peace that lingers on
Through worry, dread and even death!

He Chose Me

He chose me
As He looked down from the cross
He chose me – to live for Him

He chose me
From Calvary's hill
To give back to Him
A heart who adores

He chose me
As light for this world
Shining like the stars
Whispering of forgiveness

He chose me
Breathed love through my soul
As He rose from the tomb
On that wonderful morning

He chose me
To lift my face from fear
Feeling the serenity of hope
That faith brings deep within

He chose me
To share His heavenly home
Without any doubt
There is a day He's returning

He chose me
To go through this life
With His hand to hold me
And guide me through strife

He chose me
To listen to His word
With the assurance
That He will bring me home

He chose me
To meet Him on that day
When death rings it's bell
And I'm off to meet Him
Face to face – through eternity
Praising Him who gave me
The light to guide
The hope to provide
The faith to know
His love is the answer
To every prayer I pray

I'm so thankful
He chose me!

John 15:16
"Ye have not chosen me, but I have chosen you, and ordained you, that ye should go and bring forth fruit, and that your fruit should remain: that whatsoever ye shall ask of the Father in my name, he may give it you."

On Angel's Wings

The light of dawn lifts the dark shadows of dusk, filling the heart
with laughter that dances through the spirit in a whimsical whisper
of whirling wishes

QUOTE BY THE POET

Light dawns with a shimmering sun
Rays beam through the azure sky
Lifting the night's ebony shadows
With laughing breaths of praise

The day begins with a soothing hope
Welcoming the hues of sunny delight
Coloring the thoughts with brilliant gold
Soft amber and tones of blushing rose

Glimmering through the rays of wishes
A caress calms the heavy hearted grief
With promises of insight, inspiration,
Imagination that will always bring relief

Bright, feathery clouds pass across the blue
Racing toward the dancing whispers of noon
When robins, honey bees and butterflies
Alight upon the plumpest roses they can find

Dewy drops of liquid ride the emerald tones
Of petals bold and vibrant, rising to meet
With the loveliest breath of morning sun
Heavy with a spirit of faith that inspires dreams

Raising rich and lively dust from the forest floor
To dance around the oak, birch and sycamore
Revealing all the ways a tree can speak truth
To the heart who listens with a desire for beauty

Casting out all doubt and fear, welcoming love
That gives from the depths of the soul, singing
In poetic gasps, warming the eyes with pleasure
From knowing God is always available to protect

In the daybreak, when every thought is new
And love is as abundant as the purest star
A light flickering in the heart of those who know
This feeling of joy that comes down from above

Lighting the way with a laughing caress of hope
Sent on wings of love by God's soothing angels
Who fly across the cobalt sky, drifting down to us
In rays of haunting sunshine which melts worries
And shines through the worst of melancholy
Lighting the heart, the soul and the one who knows
God is forever the way, truth and life – shining
His light into the darkest night with wonderous insight

Wishful Thinking

If wishes fell like rain ~ then certainly I am the storm

– ANONYMOUS

Starry eyed dreamer
Filled with insight into joy
She colors the heavens
In azure laughter
Shining hues of compassion

Floating through the sky
In moments, rays break through
The dawn mists inspiration
Through the twisting ideas
Flowing into whispered tenderness

Flavoring the sunrise
With overwhelming smiles
Joyful lights that sooth the soul
With breaths of kindness
Shades of pure gold

Rain falls softly in the silence
Beating out a rhythm
Losing all thought of fear
Within the hazy harmony
Which sighs in the aroma of thrills

Joy portrays the happiness
Discovered in a touch of hope

Alive inside the faith that pours out
Delight through a heavy heart
One who beats with yearning for love

Wishes murmur through the spirit
Sending out verses of life
Energizing the inner truth, the fire
That ignites a flame of desire
Passionate poetry filled with vision

Moonbeams leave a weightless trail
Footprints echoing a prayer
For adoration which frees the mind
To reveal love for tomorrow
Faith and hope for God's promises

God is in Control

I ask God – "Why me?"
When I lose some sweet dream
What did I do to fail?
Was I wrong in some way?
Did I neglect or forsake?
Did disappointment betray?
                I ask God – "Why?"

I ask God – "When will it happen?"
Often worrying about the time
When will I get the answer . . .
To some prayer that I've prayed
Many more times than I like
Hoping for the right answer
Yet, I wait . . . stressing about the pressure

I ask God – "What should I do?"
Expecting His answer to show me
The truth, the way, the light
But I find, so many times, that
I have to struggle with patiently waiting
For the answer to come from a time
When He choses to reveal His reply

I ask God – and I sometimes question
The answer, especially if it's negative
Yet, I know, God knows the best
And I must let go and let God
If I expect to be filled with the inner
Peace that comes from knowing
God is always the One in control!

Feelings

Flowers in bright, brilliant colors
Hues of lavender, rose and scarlet
Heavenly joys planted by hands
Who know the way to the heart
Is breathed in whispers of joy
Alive, dancing with a vibrancy
That comes alive during moments
When light meets the star filled eyes

Butterflies, lighting up the morning
With breathtaking radiance, luster
Shining across the dawn like a sunrise
Welcoming the moments of hope
Inspired by feelings that flow softly
Assuring the heart that there is love
Living through all the worry and hurt
Capturing the day with an embrace

Robins and cardinals, living promises
Of the moment when hope meets honesty
And the light baths the trees in a glow
Painting the wind with a luxuriant smile
Beckoning to the soul that knows belief
Brings a gentle and wise inner serenity
Warming the feelings with a quiet strength
That radiates through sweet, loving grace

There are millions of sensations washing
The world . . . in a blushing elation that comes
Alive, like fire, desire, passion – dancing
In hope, faith and love – God's blessings
Brought down to us on the wings of angels
Who guide us in the direction of worship
Praise of the One who always makes a way

For the heart who listens to His loving direction

With a prayer filled with praise, we discover
The lasting grace that leaves us anchored
In a sense of knowing this gentle faith
That leads us quietly toward the light
Dazzling and delightful, it sets us free from
Worry, sadness and grief . . . releases us
From the pain that brings bitterness within
To the joy of love that is unconditionally given

Love like this can only be felt, never seen
It is love that comes alive with each whisper

Music in the Rain

There is silence in turmoil . . . joy in the midst of pain
Sweetness in the bitter . . . music in the rain

There is light in darkness . . . illuminated faith shines
Hues of colorful sighs . . . insights into the signs

There is beauty in unsightliness . . . kindness in the lost hope
Gentle warmth in a chill . . . that leaves a way to cope

There is laughter in the sorrow . . . mirth in the grim
Even though there is mourning . . . that leaves the eye dim

There is a whisper of inspiration . . . soothing away the cry
Allowing a tear to pierce the heart . . . mute the brightest sky

There is grace in the loathing . . . even hatred brings insight
Precious moments of understanding . . . can bring pure delight

There is goodness in the shame . . . for it means a heart is contrite
No dishonor in remorse . . . even disgrace is brighter in the moonlight

There is warmth in the winter . . . even though ice chills the bones
Fires breathe tenderness . . . to those who won't throw stones

There is caring in the selfish . . . when they mend their greed
Welcoming the attention . . . of those who are selfless indeed

There is love in the callous . . . even a hard heart can be thawed
When there is the compassion . . . to give mercy we should applaud

First, Second and Third Person

I found the joy
In light and love
Laughter sent down
From heaven above

You found the hope
In faith from the Father
A pure inspiration
From God's enlightenment

He found serenity
In a heart that gives
From the kindness within
Where heaven moves

I found joy, gladness, warmth
You found hope, healing, grace
He found peace, promise and praise

Together, we discovered
That each of our hearts
Was blessed with warmth
From the lover of our soul
The one who knows us
Better than we can grasp

Together, we learned
Life begins with it a new birth
The saving grace that gives us
A new day, a new way, a new ray
Of the Son's light coming down
To a heart who needs a real friend
And is filled with the need to see
God's grace revealed from within

The truth opens the heart's door
To wanting more and more
Of this Son's light and love
The answer sent down from above
To shower us all with good
Open the soul up to grow faithful
To the One who answers prayers
With sincerity filled with caring
Assurance filled with miracles
Second chances to be who God
Guides the heart of the convert

Together, we found the answer
To every prayer or question
This Son of God, Jesus, the Christ
Opens the way to sustaining faith
Through Grace we are saved
And through faith we can stay
Close to the Holy Spirit, the One
Who will continue to lead us home
Toward heaven, our joyful hope

Together, we know . . . God is love
And He sent His Son from above
To answer our prayer for One
Who could save us from sin and pain
Sustain us through worry and strife
Give us the assurance of a new life

Together, we three — I, You and He
Have discovered the three
The Father, Son and Holy Spirit!

I Prayed

I prayed for joy
God sent me a rainbow
Sunshine light and crimson truths
Awakening my soul to shine
As bright as the dawn

I prayed for faith
God sent me pure grace
To sustain me when I pray
And when I can't find a way
To say what I need to say

I prayed for hope
God sent me a warmth
That abides inside my soul
Coloring my world in thoughts
Of innocence, inspiration, insight

I prayed for love
God sent me a single smile
Gifted me with the pleasure of one
Who knows that the world is alive
Thriving with the dance of life

I prayed for blessings
God sent me a sense of acceptance
Of all that I encounter
Be it trial, worry or failure
He gives me His direction

I prayed for knowledge
God sent me wisdom from on high
A feeling that I could find the strength
To reach beyond my weakness

Into the heart of deepest peace

I prayed for insight
God sent me a pang of regret
A knowing that I had been selfish
With my prayers for all of these things
And I prayed . . . for someone else

God answered my prayers
With His gift of fulfillment

Just Believe

Discover joy in your heart
By listening to the
Thoughts
Of hope, faith and love
Sent down to us
From above

Joy can be found
In kindness
Seen
In a smile
Reflected
In the eyes

Joy can be found
In laughter
That denies
The sorrow
That penetrates
With grief

Joy can be found
In the presence
Of God's light
Breaking through
The darkest night

Joy can be found
In the truth felt
In a teardrop
The wonder of knowing
There is nothing
To fear
And love lives

Through every
Loss that comes near

Joy can be found
In the beauty
Of a sunny morning
In the breaking
Of the dawn
The intimacy that brings peace

God's grace gives unending joy! – Just believe

Nehemiah 8:10
Then he said unto them, Go your way, eat the fat, and drink the sweet, and send
portions unto them for whom nothing is prepared: for this day is holy unto our
Lord: neither be ye sorry; for the joy of the Lord is your strength.

The Best Bread

She won't listen
To my frustration
Blended with the exhilaration
Of being near
His precious Son
The One who gives
Us a promise of
Unending love

She doesn't value
My work and toil
And fills like she deserves
Better treatment, more worth
Than myself, who serves
With a servant's heart
Yet I feel like I'm
Last to be fed
From His spirit
The Savior's bread

She can't see
That my work is never done
I can't make her see
I need her to be
More helpful,
Useful

Mary won't listen to me
The sister who believes
In giving from my spirit
All the service I can minister

Yet, I see
She is blessed

By being
Near His breast
Where she is fed
The best bread

Luke 10
[38] Now it came to pass, as they went, that he entered into a certain village: and a certain woman named Martha received him into her house.
[39] And she had a sister called Mary, which also sat at Jesus' feet, and heard his word.
[40] But Martha was cumbered about much serving, and came to him, and said, Lord, dost thou not care that my sister hath left me to serve alone? bid her therefore that she help me.
[41] And Jesus answered and said unto her, Martha, Martha, thou art careful and troubled about many things:
[42] But one thing is needful: and Mary hath chosen that good part, which shall not be taken away from her.

She Lights the Soul

She lights up the darkest night
By giving a part of her light
To the person beside her
The one who hurts
From grief
And fights
For relief

She sparks rays of sunshine
Bright as summer
In the one who feels
Like their pain
Will never heal

She erases all doubt and fear
From the heart who lives
With the discouragement
Found inside heartbreak
Wounds that pierce
The very veins
Releasing a
Crimson flow
Of tears

She leads the trembling soul
Through the door of joy
Sending rays of hope
To caress dreams
With belief

She is one who guides an embrace
To reach out and caress
The spirit with love
Found inside

Sent from above
To fill lives
With wonder
Faith and conviction
That love is unconditional

She arouses the inspiration within
To fill the mind with serenity
That lives inside the wind
Whispering in breaths
Of gentle prayers
Sent to Him

Phillippians 2:5–7

5 Let this mind be in you, which was also in Christ Jesus:

6 Who, being in the form of God, thought it not robbery to be equal with God:

7 But made himself of no reputation, and took upon him the form of a servant, and was made in the likeness of men:

Lifelong Prayer

You grazed my heart
With tender wings
Flying high above the things
That caused me
Pain or stings

You prayed a peace
Through my dreams
Awakening love to extremes
That enlightened me
With babbling streams

You soothed my faith
With sure belief
Pledging grace, never grief
That flowed through me
Such sweet relief

You raised my hopes
With love that breathes
Affection and joy that seethes
In whispers of light
Reassuring life in wreathes

You welcomed my kindness
Through feelings of peace
Intimacy that always does increase
By the time serenity agrees
To forever find a release

You gave me a chance
To give from my very soul
Inspiration and insight that stroll

Through this life of mine
With love that makes me whole

You whispered compassion
Through my jubilant, laughing light
Shining through the dark of night
Bringing brilliant rays of faith
With a brilliant hue, so contrite

You smiled away my worries
With assurance that I am strong
Filled with wisdom and song
Living out my aspirations
With feelings blessed all lifelong

Now I Lay Me Down To Sleep

Now I lay me down to sleep . . .

I pray that God will always be there
Holding me within His loving embrace
Whispering to me of gentleness and grace
Reassuring me that I have what it takes
To reach for the stars and find the moon
Shimmering its light across my thoughts
Mysterious halo of warmth and insight

I pray that God will always let me know
When I need to give my love to someone
Who needs hope to keep moving forward
Someone who needs a kind word or deed
Something to remind them they are worthy
That God's light will shine across their life
With assurance that their faith is the answer

I pray that God will always color my thoughts
In hues of scarlet hope and sapphire trust
Breaking apart the lies of darkness and deceit
Destructive words that fall from the lips of hate
Words that are intended to discourage sweet hope
For a better day, a better way, a second chance
To give back to this world . . . hope, faith and love

I pray, now – as I lay me down to sleep . . .
For God to cover my soul – in a sanctuary
Of faith in His strength, His wisdom, His gift
Which keeps giving me the faith to move on
Past sorrow, grief and discouraging darkness
That longs to consume me so I can't see the beauty
In the morning that dawns so beautifully!

Now I lay me down to sleep . . .
Thankful that God is holding me in His palm
Reassuring me that I will come to no harm
And silencing all my worst fears or doubts
With the promise that His love answers
Every prayer!

Fake Christian

There are moments
When I find myself wishing
Yearning to be something I am not
Someone who serves Him
With never a doubt or sin
Someone who knows Him
Better than they know themselves

I wish I could say, my friend,
That I am a perfect Saint
A Christian so flawless and faultless
That I deserved the Christian name

I can't say that, my friend
For I have faults and flaws
I'm wrong sometimes and I don't always
Know the way to go
The words to say or the
Right from the wrong

I wish I could say, my friend
That I'm someone who always prays
The way that God can bless
With never a selfish desire or hope

I can't say that, though
There are times I pray for selfish gain
Times when I don't pray for the ones
That deserve the prayers the most
And times I don't seek solace
In His amazing grace

There are moments
When I find myself longing
To be someone that I can be proud of
Someone who is totally selfless
Self-sacrificing like the Savior
The One I serve in spite of the fact
That I'm so inadequate and lacking
When it comes to being a Christian

Still, I pray . . . to become like Jesus
The One I know can take this clay I am
And create someone worthy of His love

I'm not a fake Christian
But I am a Christian who knows
I'm not perfect – even though I want to be
More like my Savior
Jesus, who died for me!

Strength in Weakness

You love me, even when I am wrong
A sinner, frail and weak, in search of a song
Reaching out to the joys I sometimes see
In hearts who give without condition or plea
You love me, and it is such a sweet mystery
Knowing that this hope will go down in history
For the wonderous inspiration that fulfills
Imagination and purpose that enlivens and thrills
You love me, in spite of all that I have done
To discourage your love, the embrace homespun
With my worries, struggles and cynicism
All those things that assure my criticism
You love me, although I'm not always endearing
Leaving me with hope that won't be disappearing
Creating a wellspring of compassion within me
That fills me with assurance that I'm finally free
You love me, and give me grace everlasting
Always securing me so that I never feel contrasting
But always know the beauty of my dreams
Will hold me in a embrace like the soft sunbeams
You love me, calming my worst sorrows and pains
Soothing away the trials that leave me in chains
Breaking away pieces of anguish that destroys my best
Reminding me that I am most assuredly blessed
You love me through the troubles and adversities
Coloring my ideas with passions and diversities
Reflecting on all the faith I have known because of You
The Jesus who taught me to give, live and pursue
Goodness, acceptance, gentleness and meekness
Which come from Him who gives strength in weakness

2 Corinthians 12:9 — And he said unto me, My grace is sufficient for thee: for my strength is made perfect in weakness. Most gladly therefore will I rather glory in my infirmities, that the power of Christ may rest upon me.

A Silent Teardrop

Falling silent against naked cheek . . .

When an emotion stuns or stings
Cutting through the composure
To free the heart of liquid poison
Toxic feelings of pain and sorrow
Grief that slashes through self-control
Leaving the heart in deep discouragement
Touching thoughts with negativity
That comes from a lack of sensitivity
Lighting the way to eventual joy
That comes when one finally lets go
Of sorrow, sadness, anguish
All the feelings that bring heartache
To the one who listens to the beating
The throbbing and pounding, the breath
Of a silent tear, reflecting the soul
Who knows only angst and pain
Beliefs colored in hues of ebony
Dark thoughts, black coats of sorrow
That change dreams to nightmares
Hopes to desperateness and misery
A sting that eventually lacerates
The faith that sustains and remains
Even after the sorrow and pain
Brings a teardrop to cling to the face
Who floods the spirit with shame
From allowing the heart to hold onto
A flow of disdain, grief and woe
That is engrained in the one who knows
A silent tear is sometimes the answer
To a prayer for relief to this agony!

A Light From the Son

I mouth a prayer for hope and healing
Feelings of doubt so often plague me
With their skepticism and suspicion
Their hesitancy and apprehension
The plagues of worry and superstition
Coming from a tormenting thought
Lies spoken by the enemy
Who encourages mistrust
Cynicism and disbelief
Suspecting love
Of grief

I mouth a prayer for kindness
Whispers of sweet inspiration
Joy that peppers my ideas
And answers me with
Creativity and peace
Assurance that I have
What it takes to give
The gift of love
From within
Where I am
Only me

I mouth a prayer of longing for wisdom
Promises of truths that abide within
Coloring my heart in hues of
Crimson pleasure, thrilling
Reflections that sooth
And soften the heart
With a sense of charity
That gives fully

Unconditionally
With a love
That never
Ends

I mouth a prayer for God's blessings
To sustain and reflect goodness
Within our spirits, our souls
Where light and love flow
In breaths of fiery passion
That blows through
The thoughts,
In waves of
Desire that
Enchants
And grants
Adoration
For His
Son

The One I worship and know
As my guiding light
My echo of peace
My enlightenment
My faith in grace
The answer to all my prayers
For love that abides
Deep within
My soul
Shining
Out

A sparkle of hope
In the dark
Like a star, like the moon
Lighting the way to truth
It is this love that lives

To reveal to us
The One who instills in us
Unconditional love
From above

A light from the Son

Made in the USA
Coppell, TX
17 January 2022

71721662R10134